Student Solutions M[anual]

for use with

Essentials of Econometrics

Third Edition

Damodar N. Gujarati
United States Military Academy, West Point

Prepared by
Damodar N. Gujarati
with the assistance of Andrew Paizis

McGraw-Hill Irwin

Boston   Burr Ridge, IL   Dubuque, IA   Madison, WI   New York   San Francisco   St. Louis
Bangkok   Bogotá   Caracas   Kuala Lumpur   Lisbon   London   Madrid   Mexico City
Milan   Montreal   New Delhi   Santiago   Seoul   Singapore   Sydney   Taipei   Toronto

McGraw-Hill Irwin

Student Solutions Manual for use with
ESSENTIALS OF ECONOMETRICS
Damodar N. Gujarati

Published by McGraw-Hill/Irwin, an imprint of The McGraw-Hill Companies, Inc., 1221 Avenue of the Americas, New York, NY 10020. Copyright © 2006, 2003, 2001 by The McGraw-Hill Companies, Inc. All rights reserved.

No part of this publication may be reproduced or distributed in any form or by any means, or stored in a database or retrieval system, without the prior written consent of The McGraw-Hill Companies, Inc., including, but not limited to, in any network or other electronic storage or transmission, or broadcast for distance learning.

1 2 3 4 5 6 7 8 9 0 QSR/QSR 0 9 8 7 6 5

ISBN 0-07-304209-9

www.mhhe.com

The McGraw-Hill Companies

TABLE OF CONTENTS

Preface:		iv
CHAPTER 1:	The Nature and Scope of Econometrics	1

PART ONE: BASICS OF PROBABILITY AND STATISTICS

CHAPTER 2:	Review of Statistics: Probability and Probability Distributions	9
CHAPTER 3:	Characteristics of Probability Distributions	14
CHAPTER 4:	Some Important Probability Distributions	21
CHAPTER 5:	Statistical Inference: Estimation and Hypothesis Testing	26

PART TWO: THE LINEAR REGRESSION MODEL

CHAPTER 6:	Basic Ideas of Linear Regression: The Two-Variable Model	31
CHAPTER 7:	The Two-Variable Model: Hypothesis Testing	44
CHAPTER 8:	Multiple Regression: Estimation and Hypothesis Testing	56
CHAPTER 9:	Functional Forms of Regression Models	66
CHAPTER 10:	Dummy Variable Regression Models	79

PART THREE: REGRESSION ANALYSIS IN PRACTICE

CHAPTER 11:	Model Selection: Criteria and Tests	91
CHAPTER 12:	Multicollinearity: What Happens if Explanatory Variables are Correlated?	101
CHAPTER 13:	Heteroscedasticity: What Happens if the Error Variance is Nonconstant?	110
CHAPTER 14:	Autocorrelation: What Happens if Error Terms are Correlated?	121

PART FOUR: ADVANCED TOPICS IN ECONOMETRICS

CHAPTER 15:	Simultaneous Equation Models	129
CHAPTER 16:	Selected Topics in Single Equation Regression Models	133

PREFACE

This manual provides detailed solutions to all the questions and problems given in *Essentials of Econometrics*. Answers to some of the questions are subjective and the instructor may want to inject his/her own views in these questions. Providing answers to numerical questions has been a tedious and time-consuming task. I am deeply indebted to Andrew Paizis for checking answers to all the questions and problems. However, it is likely that some errors have crept in inadvertently. I would appreciate it very much if the reader will bring them to my attention. I will post all the corrections on the book's web site. Please check the web site from time to time. It is: www.mhhe.com/economics/gujaratiess3

I would welcome any comments, criticisms, or suggestions that you may have to improve the quality of the questions and problems. Finding concrete economic and business data sets is a challenging task. I would, therefore, welcome any data sets that you may have which they would like to share with me. Of course, I will give the appropriate credit.

I am looking forward to hearing from you.

Damodar Gujarati
Professor of Economics
U.S. Military Academy
West Point, NY 10996
Jd8347@usma.edu

CHAPTER 1

THE NATURE AND SCOPE OF ECONOMETRICS

QUESTIONS

1.1. (**a**) Other things remaining the same, the higher the tax rate is, the lower the price of a house will be.

(**b**) Assume that the data are cross-section, involving several residential communities with differing tax rates.

(**c**) $Y_i = B_1 + B_2 X_i$

where Y = price of the house and X = tax rate

(**d**) $Y_i = B_1 + B_2 X_i + u_i$

(**e**) Given the sample, one can use OLS to estimate the parameters of the model.

(**f**) Aside from the tax rate, other factors that affect house prices are mortgage interest rates, house size, buyers' family income, the state of the economy, the local crime rate, etc. Such variables may be included in a more detailed multiple regression model.

(**g**) *A priori*, $B_2 < 0$. Therefore, one can test $H_0 : B_2 \geq 0$ against $H_1 : B_2 < 0$.

(**h**) The estimated regression can be used to predict the average price of a house in a community, given the tax rate in that community. Of course, it is assumed that all other factors stay the same.

1.2. Econometricians are now routinely employed in government and business to estimate and / or forecast (1) price and cost elasticities, (2) production and cost functions, and (3) demand functions for goods and services, etc. Econometric forecasting is a growth industry.

1.3. The economy will be bolstered if the increase in the money supply leads to a reduction in the interest rate which will lead to more investment activity and, therefore, to more output and more employment. If the increase in the money supply, however, leads to inflation, the preceding result may not occur. The job of the econometrician will be to develop a model to predict the effect of the increase in the money supply on inflation, interest rate, employment, etc.

1.4. As a matter of fact, on October 1, 1993 the Federal Government did increase the gasoline tax by 4 cents. Since gasoline and cars are complementary products, economic theory suggests that an increase in the price of gasoline will not only lead to a decline in the demand for gasoline but also in the demand for cars, *ceteris paribus*. The Ford Motor Company may be advised to produce more fuel-efficient cars to stave off a serious decline in the demand for its cars. An automobile demand function will provide numerical estimates of the effect of gasoline tax on the demand for automobiles.

1.5. As a pure economist, you will advise against imposing such a tariff, for it will not only increase the price of imported steel but will also increase the prices of all goods that use imported steel, especially the prices of automobiles. It will also protect inefficient domestic producers of steel.

The best way to set up an econometric model would be to look at past episodes of tariffs and see their impact on various products, pre- and post- the imposition of such tariffs.

PROBLEMS

1.6. (*a*) The plot will show that both the CPI and the S&P 500 stock index generally show an upward trend, whereas the three-month Treasury bill rate is generally downward trending.

(Graphs appear in the following pages)

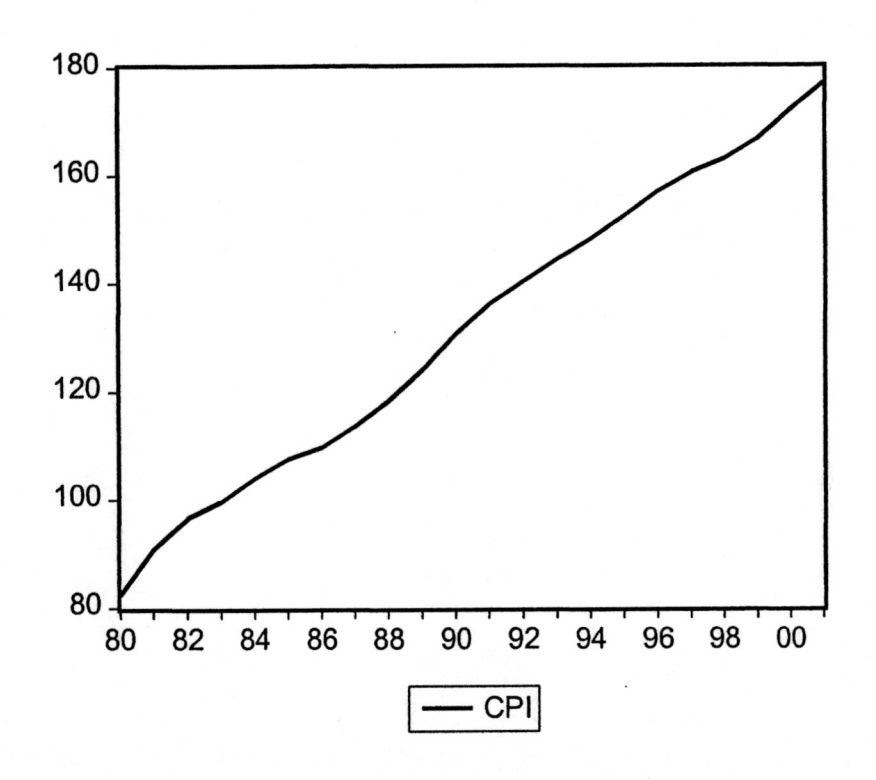

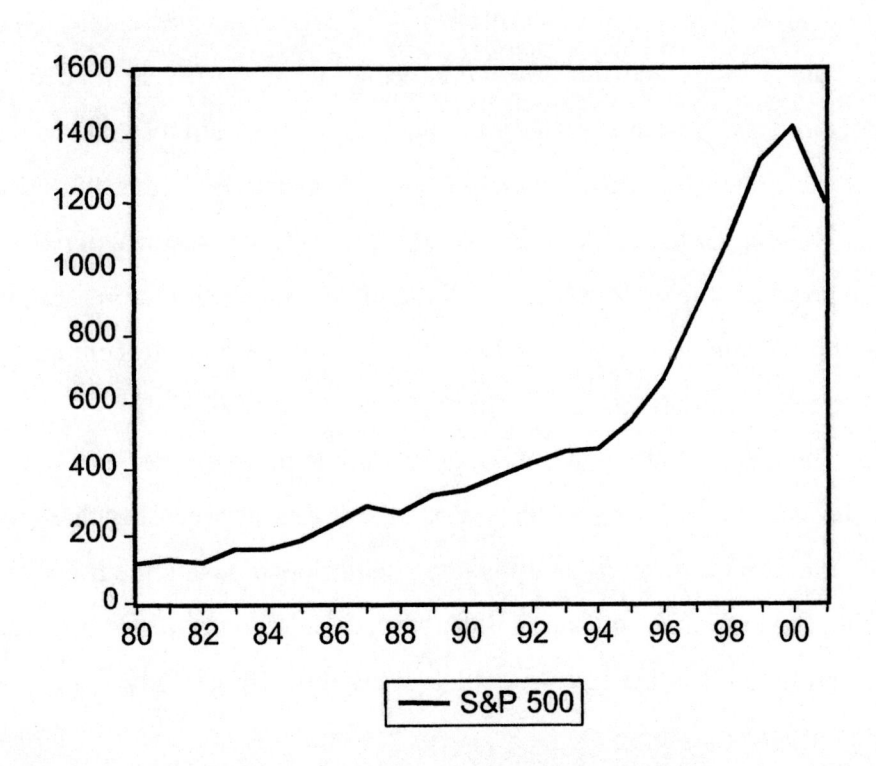

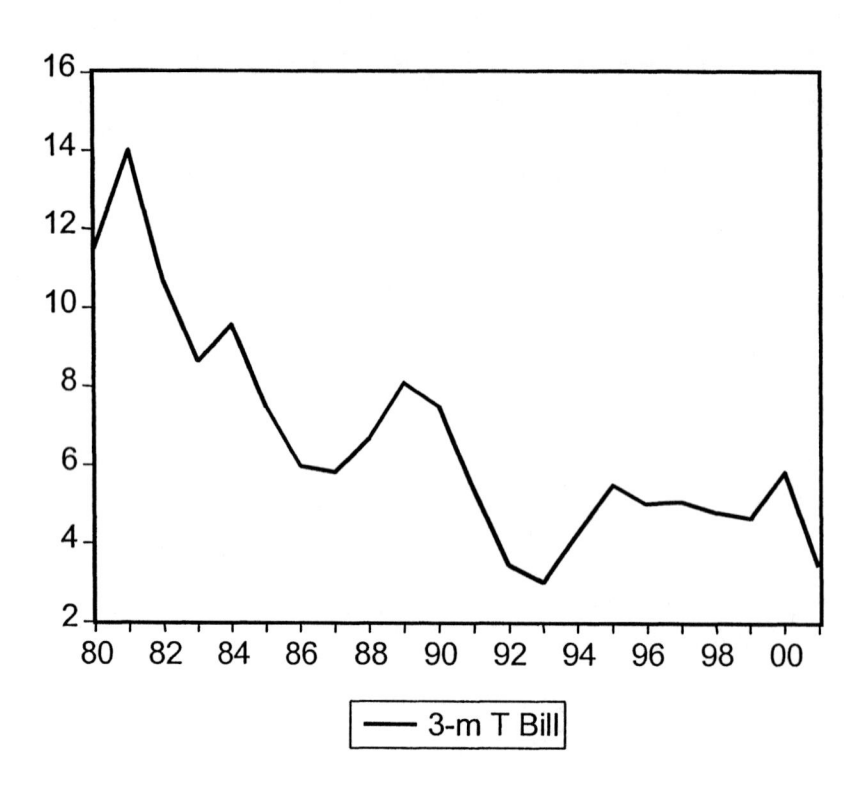

(b) If investment in the stock market is a hedge against inflation, the S&P 500 stock index and the CPI are expected to be positively related. The three-month Treasury bill rate is expected to be positively related to the inflation rate according the *Fisher effect*, because the higher the inflation rate, the higher the nominal rate of interest that the investor will expect. In the problem, the price variable is the CPI and not the inflation rate (which is the percentage change in the CPI): So the appropriate comparison is between the inflation rate and the three-month Treasury bill.

(c) The data will show that the regression line between the S&P 500 stock index and the CPI is positively sloped, but that between the three-month Treasury bill rate and the CPI is negatively sloped. Using the inflation rate instead of the CPI, the data will show that the regression line between the inflation rate and the three-month Treasury bill is positively sloped, as the *Fisher effect* is stating.

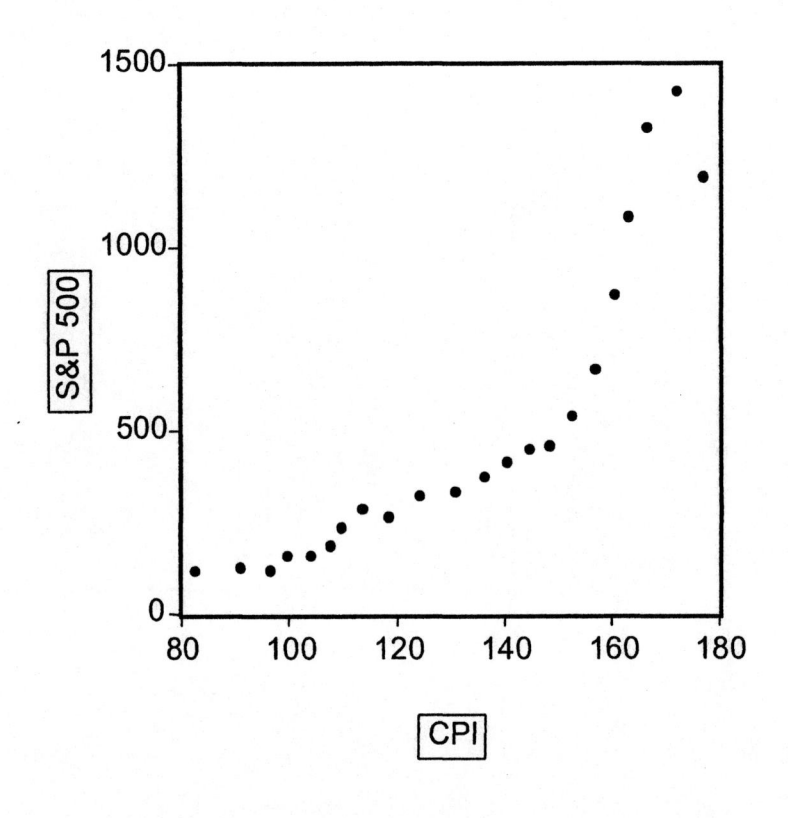

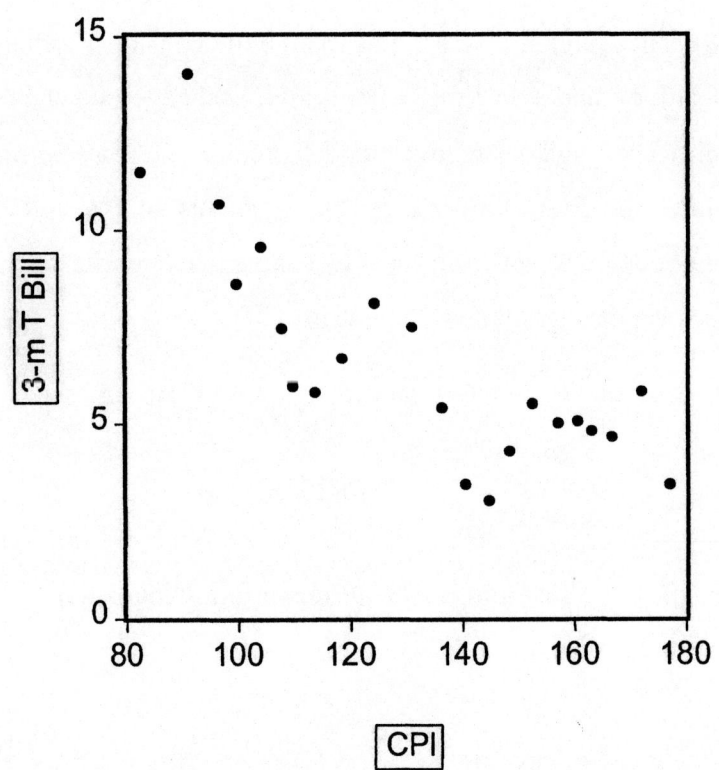

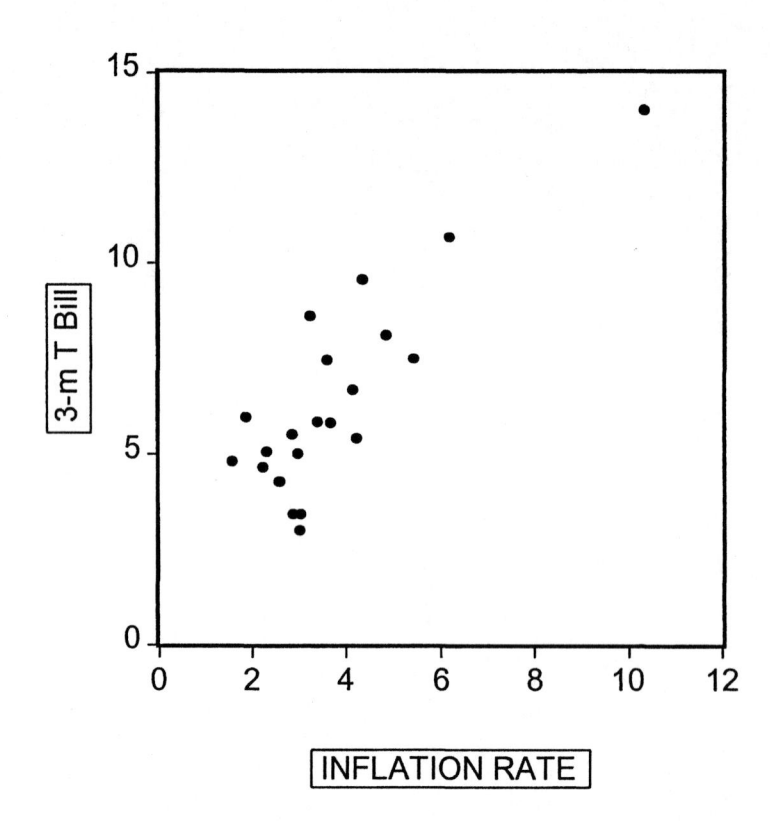

1.7. **(a)** The diagrams will show that both consumer price indexes show a positive trend over time, whereas the exchange rate shows a positive trend until 1985 and a negative trend thereafter. It may be noted that in 1985, under the *Plaza Accord,* the governments of the G-7 countries made a deliberate attempt to bring down the exchange rate of the dollar vis-à-vis the currencies of the G-7 countries.

(Graphs appear on the following page)

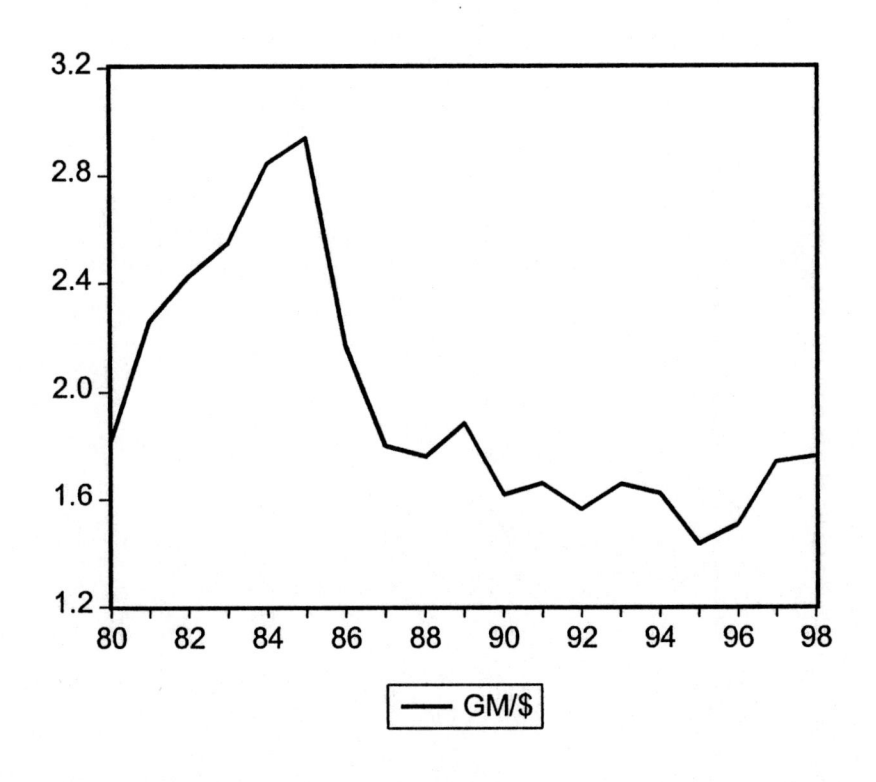

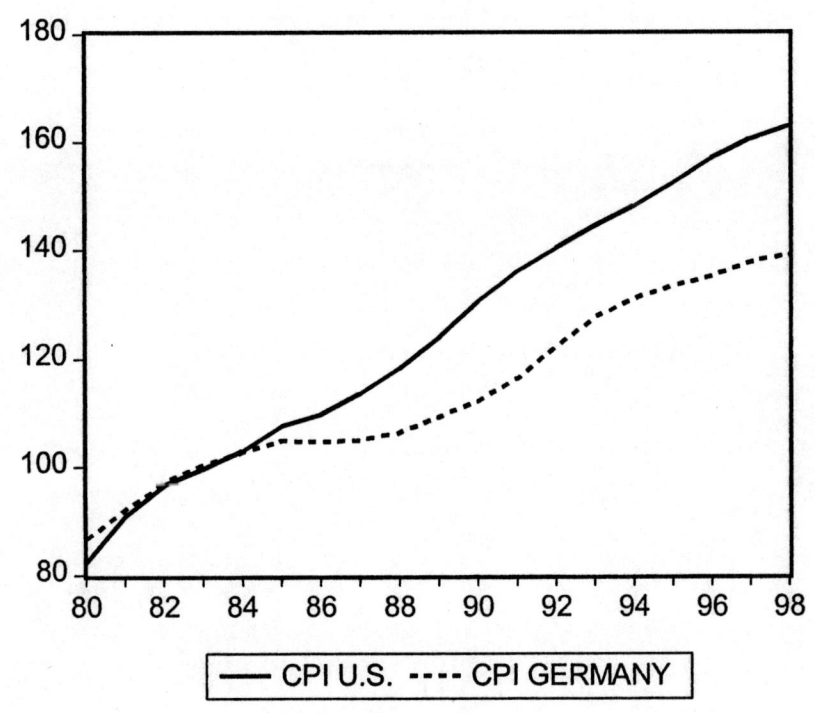

(b), **(c)**, and **(d)**: The plot of the ER (GM/$) against the RPR will show a positive relationship between the two until 1985 but a negative relationship thereafter.

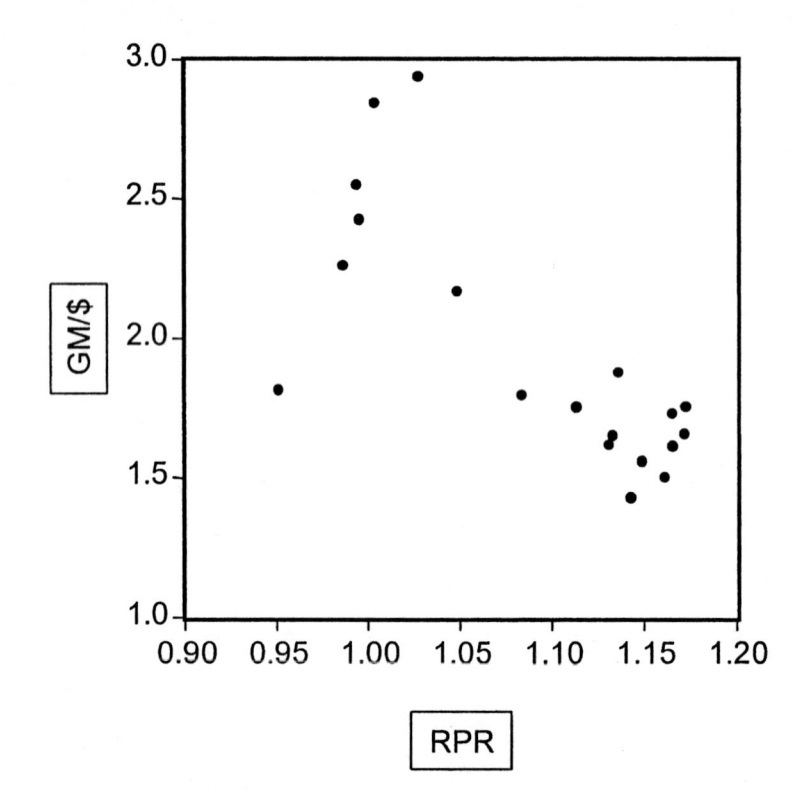

CHAPTER 2

REVIEW OF STATISTICS: PROBABILITY AND PROBABILITY DISTRIBUTIONS

QUESTIONS

2.1. See Sections 2.2, 2.4, 2.5, and 2.6.

2.2. No. Notice that a pair of events, A and B, are mutually exclusive if they cannot occur jointly, that is, $P(AB) = 0$. Independence, on the other hand, means that $P(AB) = P(A) P(B)$. Consider this example. Let A = the card is a heart and B = the card is an ace. A card is drawn from a deck of 52 cards. We know that $P(A) = 1/4$ and that $P(B) = 1/13$. The probability of the event that a card is both a heart and an ace is $P(AB) = 1/52 = P(A) P(B)$. Hence the two events are independent. But they are not mutually exclusive because the ace of hearts could be drawn.

2.3. (*a*) True, (*b*) True.

2.4. (*a*) Yes, they are also collectively exhaustive.

(*b*) (*i*) Events E_1 and A_2 occur together, (*ii*) events E_3 or A_3 occur,

(*iii*) E_1 or A_1 occur and similarly for the other three combinations;

(*iv*) events $E_2 A_1$, $E_3 A_2$, $E_4 A_3$ occur (Each pair occurs together).

Note that forecasts and actual events need not coincide. It is possible that E_1 was predicted, but the actual growth was A_4 and vice versa.

2.5. PDF relates to a continuous variable and PMF to a discrete variable.

2.6. The CDF of a discrete variable is a step function, whereas that of a continuous variable is a continuous curve.

2.7. Making the substitution, we obtain $P(A|B) = \dfrac{P(B|A)P(A)}{P(B)}$. This is simply *Bayes'* formula. If we think of *A* as a possible hypothesis about some phenomenon, *Bayes' theorem* shows how opinions about this hypothesis held *a priori* should be modified in light of actual experience. In Bayesian language, $P(A)$ is known as *prior* probability and $P(A|B)$ is known as *posterior* (or revised) probability.

PROBLEMS

2.8. (a) $\sum_{i=1}^{4} x^{i-1} = x^0 + x + x^2 + x^3$ (Note: $x^0 = 1$).

(b) $\sum_{i=2}^{6} ay_i = a \sum_{i=2}^{6} y_i = a(y_2 + y_3 + y_4 + y_5 + y_6)$

(c) $\sum_{i=1}^{2} (2x_i + 3y_i) = 2\sum_{i=1}^{2} x_i + 3\sum_{i=1}^{2} y_i = 2(x_1 + x_2) + 3(y_1 + y_2)$

(d) $\sum_{i=1}^{3} \sum_{j=1}^{2} x_i y_j = x_1 y_1 + x_2 y_1 + x_3 y_1 + x_1 y_2 + x_2 y_2 + x_3 y_2$

(e) $\sum_{i=1}^{4} i + 4 = \sum_{i=1}^{4} i + \sum_{i=1}^{4} 4 = (1 + 2 + 3 + 4) + (4)(4) = 26$

(f) $\sum_{i=1}^{3} 3^i = 3 + 3^2 + 3^3 = 39$

(g) $\sum_{i=1}^{10} 2 = (2)(10) = 20$

(h) $\sum_{x=1}^{3} (4x^2 - 3) = 4\sum_{x=1}^{3} x^2 - \sum_{x=1}^{3} 3 = 4(1^2 + 2^2 + 3^2) - (3)(3) = 47$

2.9. (a) $\sum_{i=1}^{5} x_i$ (i from 1 to 5)

(b) $\sum_{i=1}^{5} i\, x_i$ (i from 1 to 5)

(c) $\sum_{i=1}^{k} (x_i^2 + y_i^2)$ (i from 1 to k)

2.10. (a) $[500\,(500 + 1)] / 2 = 125{,}250$

(b) $\sum_{1}^{100} k - \sum_{1}^{9} k = [100\,(101)] / 2 - [9\,(10)] / 2 = 5{,}005$

(c) $3\sum_{10}^{100} k = 3(5{,}005) = 15{,}015$, using (b) above.

2.11. (a) $[10(11)(21)]/6 = 385$

(b) $\sum_{1}^{20} k^2 - \sum_{1}^{9} k^2 = \frac{20(21)(41)}{6} - \frac{9(10)(19)}{6} = 2{,}585$

(c) $\sum_{1}^{19} k^2 - \sum_{1}^{10} k^2 = \frac{19(20)(39)}{6} - \frac{10(11)(21)}{6} = 2{,}085$

(d) $4\sum_{1}^{10} k^2 = 4(385) = 1{,}540$, using (a) above.

2.12. (a) Since $\sum f(X) = 1$, $(b + 2b + 3b + 4b + 5b) = 15b = 1$. Therefore, we have $b = 1/15$.

(b) $P(X \le 2) = 6/15$; $P(X \le 3) = 10/15$; $P(2 \le X \le 3) = 4/15$

2.13. (a) Marginal distributions:

X	1	2	3
f(X)	0.20	0.40	0.40

Y	1	2	3	4
f(Y)	0.15	0.10	0.45	0.30

(b) Conditional distributions:

f(X|Y)	f(Y|X)
$P(X=1 \mid Y=1) = 0.03/0.15 = 0.20$	$P(Y=1 \mid X=1) = 0.03/0.20 = 0.15$
$P(X=2 \mid Y=1) = 0.06/0.15 = 0.40$	$P(Y=2 \mid X=1) = 0.02/0.20 = 0.10$
$P(X=3 \mid Y=1) = 0.06/0.15 = 0.40$	$P(Y=3 \mid X=1) = 0.09/0.20 = 0.45$
……….	$P(Y=4 \mid X=1) = 0.06/0.20 = 0.30$
……….	……….

The remaining conditional distributions can be derived similarly.

2.14. Let B represent the event that a person reads the *Wall Street Journal* and let A_1, A_2, and A_3 denote, respectively, the events a Democrat, a Republican, and an Independent. We want to find out $P(A_2 \mid B)$:

$$P(A_2|B) = \frac{P(B|A_2)P(A_2)}{P(B|A_2)P(A_2)+P(B|A_1)P(A_1)+P(B|A_3)P(A_3)}$$

$$= \frac{(0.6)(0.4)}{(0.6)(0.4)+(0.3)(0.5)+(0.4)(0.1)} = 0.558$$

Note that the prior probability of sampling a Republican is 0.4 or 40%. But knowing that someone is found reading the *Wall Street Journal*, the probability of sampling a Republican increases to 0.558 or 55.8%. This makes sense, for it has been observed that proportionately more Republicans than Democrats or Independents read the *Journal*. This example is an illustration of *Bayes' Theorem*.

2.15. This is $P(A+B)$ or $P(A \cup B) = 0.9$.

2.16. (*a*) No, for the probability that this happens is 0.2 and not zero.

(*b*) Let A denote having children and B denote work outside home. If these two events are to be independent, we must have $P(AB) = P(A)\,P(B)$. In the present case, $P(AB) = 0.2$ and $P(A) = 0.5$ and $P(B) = 0.6$. Since in this case $P(AB) \neq P(A)\,P(B)$, the two events are not independent.

2.17. From Table 2-9, it can be seen that

X→ Y↓	Below poverty	Above poverty	f(Y) ↓
White	0.08	0.67	**0.75**
Black	0.03	0.09	**0.12**
Hispanic	0.03	0.10	**0.13**
f(X) →	**0.14**	**0.86**	**1.00**

(*a*) $f(X|Y=\text{White}) = \dfrac{f(X,Y=\text{White})}{f(Y=\text{White})} = \dfrac{0.08}{0.75} \approx 0.1067$

$f(X|Y=\text{Black}) = \dfrac{f(X,Y=\text{Black})}{f(Y=\text{Black})} = \dfrac{0.03}{0.12} = 0.2500$

$$f(X|Y=Hispanic) = \frac{f(X,Y=Hispanic)}{f(Y=Hispanic)} = \frac{0.03}{0.13} \approx 0.2308$$

(b) They are not. For them to be independent, $f(X,Y) = f(X)f(Y)$ must hold true for all combinations of X and Y values, which is not the case here.

2.18. **(a)** For it to be a proper PDF, we must have $c\int_0^2 (4x-2x^2)dx = 1$. That is,

$c\left[\frac{4}{2}x^2 - \frac{2}{3}x^3\right]_0^2 = 1$. That is, $c\left(\frac{16}{2} - \frac{16}{3}\right) = 1$, or $\frac{8}{3}c = 1$, which gives $c = \frac{3}{8}$.

(b) $\frac{3}{8}\int_1^2 (4x-2x^2)dx = \frac{3}{8}\left[\frac{4}{2}x^2 - \frac{2}{3}x^3\right]_1^2 = \frac{3}{8}\left(\frac{4}{3}\right) = \frac{1}{2}$.

(c) $P(x>2) = 1 - P(x<2) = 1 - \frac{3}{8}\int_0^2 (4x-2x^2)dx = 1 - 1 = 0$.

2.19. **(a)** $f(x) = \int_0^1 \frac{12}{5}(2x-x^2-xy)dy = \frac{18}{5}x - \frac{12}{5}x^2$.

Therefore, $P(x>0.5) = 1 - P(x<0.5) = 1 - \int_0^{0.5}\left(\frac{18}{5}x - \frac{12}{5}x^2\right)dx = 0.65$.

Following a similar procedure, you can verify that $P(y<0.5) = 0.65$.

(b) $f(x|y) = \frac{f(x,y)}{f(y)} = \frac{f(x,y)}{\int_0^1 f(x,y)dx} = \frac{x(2-x-y)}{\int_0^1 x(2-x-y)dx} = \frac{x(2-x-y)}{\frac{2}{3} - \frac{y}{2}}$

$= \frac{6x(2-x-y)}{4-3y}$.

CHAPTER 3

CHARACTERISTICS OF PROBABILITY DISTRIBUTIONS

QUESTIONS

3.1. Summary characteristics of a PDF are known as moments. The most commonly encountered moments are the mean, variance and covariance. The mean value is known as the first moment, the variance is known as the second moment, etc. In general, the rth moment of a random variable X around its mean value, μ_x, is defined as $m_r = E(X - \mu_x)^1$. For $r = 1$, we obtain the first moment, which is the mean value; for $r = 2$, we obtain the second moment, which is the variance; for $r = 3$ we obtain the third moment, and so on.

3.2. (*a*) A measure of central tendency (i.e., center of gravity) in the distribution of a random variable.

(*b*) A measure of spread or dispersion in the distribution of a random variable.

(*c*) The (positive) square of variance, also a measure of spread in the distribution of a random variable.

(*d*) A measure of (linear) association between two random variables.

(*e*) Also a measure of linear association between two random variables that is independent of the units of measurement and always lies between -1 and 1.

(*f*) The expected value of a random variable that may depend on the values of one or more other variables.

3.3. (*a*) to (*e*). These are the sample counterparts of the concepts discussed in Question 3.2.

3.4. In practice one relies on the data drawn from some population, for one does rarely obtain the data on the whole population or even if one could get it, it would be very expensive to collect that information. A lot of homeless people live in the streets of Manhattan, but it is very difficult to track them down. Most studies on the homeless are based on a sample of such people.

3.5 (*a*) This is already shown in the question.

(b) .... variability or spread around the expected value.

(c) .... linear association between two random variables.

(d) .... linear association between two random variables, except that it is free of units of measurement and always lies between -1 and 1.

3.6. Yes, because it is a squared quantity.

3.7. **(a)** *True*, which is obvious from the definition of the variance of a random variable.

(b) *True.* The covariance can be positive or negative, but the standard deviation always takes a positive value. Then, it is clear from the formula used to compute the correlation coefficient that it will have the same sign as that of the covariance between two variables.

(c) *False.* Only when the two variables are independent, it will be true.

(d) *True.* If two variables X and Y are independent, $E(XY) = E(X) E(Y) = \mu_x \mu_y$. Substituting this in formula (3.23) the conclusion follows.

(e) *False* generally. Let $Y = X^2$ and let the r.v. X take the values of -1, 0, and 1 with probabilities of 0.25, 0.50, and 0.25, respectively. If you compute the covariance between Y and X, you will find that it is zero. But we know that Y and X are not independent. The reason why this statement is generally false is that the covariance is a measure of linear dependence between two random variables. In the present example, however, Y and X are non-linearly related. The only exception to the rule is if X and Y are jointly normally distributed, in which case zero covariance implies independence.

(f) *False.* The expectation operator E is a linear operator. It is not applicable to nonlinear functions, such as $(1/X)$.

(g) *False.* $E[X-\mu_x]^2$ on the left-hand-side of the expression is the variance of the random variable X and is always a positive quantity. Since $E(X-\mu_x)$ is always zero, the right-hand-expression is meaningless. Note that

$$E(X-\mu_x) = E(X) - E(\mu_x) = \mu_x - \mu_x = 0.$$

PROBLEMS

3.8   (a) $40/15 \cong 2.67$

    (b) $130/15 - (40/15)^2 = 1.5556$; s.d. $= 1.2472$

    (c) $V = \dfrac{\sigma_X}{\mu_X} 100 = \dfrac{1.2472}{2.67} 100 \approx 46.71\%$

    (d) Skewness: $S = -1.1407 / 1.9401 \approx -0.5880$

        Kurtosis: $K = 5.4962 / 2.4198 \approx 2.2714$

3.9.   (a) $E(X) = \sum x_i P(X_i = x_i) = 8.75\%$

    (b) $\text{var}(X) = \sum [X - E(X)]^2 P(X = x_i) = 224.6875$ (percent squared)

        s.d. $(X) = \sqrt{224.6875} = 14.99\%$

    (c) Skewness: $S = -1{,}811.72 / 3{,}367.97 = -0.5379$, negatively skewed.

        Kurtosis: $K = 114{,}488.77 / 50{,}484.47 = 2.2678$, platykurtic.

    (d) The CDF is:

X	-20	-10	10	25	30
f(X)	0.10	0.15	0.45	0.25	0.05
F(X)	0.10	0.25	0.70	0.95	1.00

    From this it follows that $P(\leq 10) = 0.70$.

3.10.   (a) The marginal distributions are:

X	-10	0	20	30
f(X)	0.27	0.12	0.26	0.35

Y	20	50
f(Y)	0.51	0.49

    (b) $E(Y) = 34.7\%$

    (c) $f(Y = 20 | X = 20) = \dfrac{f(Y = 20, X = 20)}{f(X = 20)} = \dfrac{0.16}{0.26} \approx 0.6154$

        $f(Y = 50 | X = 20) = \dfrac{f(Y = 50, X = 20)}{f(X = 20)} = \dfrac{0.10}{0.26} \approx 0.3846$

(d) $E(XY) = 635 \neq E(X) E(Y) = 451.1$. Hence, the two rates of return are not independent.

3.11. **(a)** $E(Y) = E(3X + 2) = 3 E(X) + 2 = 26$

var $(Y) =$ var $(3X + 2) = 9$ var$(X) = 36$

(b) $E(Y) = E(0.6X - 4) = 0.6 E(X) - 4 = 0.8$

var $(Y) =$ var $(0.6X - 4) = 0.36$ var $(X) = 1.44$

(c) $E(X/4) = 1/4\, E(X) = 2$

var $(X/4) = 1/16$ var $(X) = 1/4$

(d) $E(Y) = E(aX + b) = a E(X) + b = 8a + b$

var$(Y) = a^2$ var $(X) = 4 a^2$

(e) $Y = E(3X^2 + 2) = 3E(X^2) + 2$. From Equation (3.18), we observe that

$E(X^2) = \text{var}(X) + [E(X)]^2 = 4 + 8^2 = 68$. Therefore,

$E(3X^2 + 2) = 68 + 2 = 70$.

var$(Y) =$ var $(3X^2 + 2) = 9$ var(X^2)

3.12. var $(X + Y) = 16 + 9 + 2(-0.8)(4)(3) = 5.8$, which Is smaller than the sum of var $(X) +$ var $(Y) = 25$.

If an investment is made equally in the two securities, we have:

var $(1/2\, X + 1/2\, Y) = 1/4$ var $(X) + 1/4$ var $(Y) + (-0.8)(4/2)(3/2) = 3.85$.

This variance is obviously smaller than either variance individually. Therefore, it pays to diversify.

3.13. **(a)** Average value $= 683{,}939.1$; variance $= (41{,}167.5)^2$

(b) Average value $= 67{,}857.6$; variance $= (15{,}200.1)^2$

(c) Covariance $= 45{,}932{,}190.7$; correlation coefficient $= 0.0734$

Note: This covariance, $45{,}932{,}190.7$, is a sample covariance. Microsoft *Excel* and *EViews* have their own automatic covariance options but their default assumption is that the data are a population. Therefore, using these automatic options will result in a different covariance number. The answer shown here was calculated manually in Excel by dividing the product of the deviations from the means of X and Y by $n - 1 = 11$, as it is appropriate for a sample.

(d) Since the covariance between the two is positive, it seems that the two variables are not independent.

(e) No, because correlation does not imply causation.

3.14. $\text{var}(X+Y) = \text{var}(X) + \text{var}(Y) + 2\text{cov}(X,Y)$
$= \text{var}(X) + \text{var}(Y) + 2[E(XY) - E(X)E(Y)]$.

First, compute $E(X), E(Y), \text{var}(X), \text{var}(Y)$ and $E(XY)$ from the data given in Table 2-7. We obtain:

$E(X) = 2.20; E(Y) = 2.90, \text{var}(X) = 0.56; \text{var}(Y) = 0.99; E(XY) = 6.38$.

Hence, $\text{var}(X+Y) = 0.56 + 0.99 + 2[6.38 - (2.20)(2.90)] = 1.55$

As you can see, the variance of the sum of X and Y is larger than the variance of either variable.

3.15 (a) cov(S&P500, CPI)) = 9,965.380; cov(MTB3, CPI) = - 62.0063. These are sample covariances.

Note: Although the data are a sample, and the above covariances are called sample covariances, the actual numbers shown here were generated with the automatic *Excel* and *EViews* covariance options, meaning the numbers were calculated under the population assumption. See Problem 3.13 (c) above.

(b) corr(S&P500, CPI) = 0.8899; corr(MTB3, CPI) = -0.8078. *A priori*, the correlation between the S&P500 and the CPI is expected to be positive if investment in the stock market is a hedge against inflation. *A priori*, the correlation between the *inflation rate* and three-month Treasury bill is also expected to be positive, a la the *Fisher effect*. The negative correlation between the MTB3 and the CPI does not invalidate the *Fisher effect*: The appropriate measure is the inflation rate (percentage change in the CPI). In fact, corr(Inflation Rate, MTB3) = 0.8440. See also Problem 1.6 (b) and (c).

(c) Remember that correlation does not necessarily imply causation.

3.16 Since the exchange rate is defined as the number of German Marks per US dollar and since the relative price is defined as the ratio of the US CPI to German CPI, the correlation between the two is expected to be negative. This makes sense because if the US CPI goes up relative to the German CPI, the exchange rate is expected to depreciate, that is, a dollar will buy fewer Marks than before. The value of the correlation coefficient is -0.7454. By the same analysis, the correlation between the exchange rate and the inverse of relative prices is expected to be positive, which is in fact the case. The value of this correlation is 0.7320.

OPTIONAL EXERCISES

3.17. $E(X) = \int_0^3 X \frac{X^2}{9} dx = \frac{1}{9}\int_0^3 X^3 dx = \frac{1}{9}\left[\frac{X^4}{4}\right]_0^3 = 2.25$

3.18. (*a*) $\text{var}(X) = E(X^2) - [E(X)]^2 > 0$, since the variance is always positive. Therefore, $E(X^2) > [E(X)]^2$. In words, the expected value of the square of X is greater than the squared value of the expected value of X.

(*b*) By definition, we have:
$$\text{cov}(X,Y) = E\{[(X-E(X)][Y-E(Y)]\}$$
$$= E(XY - X\mu_Y - Y\mu_X + \mu_X\mu_Y)$$
$$= E(XY) - \mu_Y E(X) - \mu_X E(Y) + \mu_X\mu_Y$$
$$= E(XY) - \mu_X\mu_Y - \mu_X\mu_Y + \mu_X\mu_Y = E(XY) - \mu_X\mu_Y.$$

Note that μ_X and μ_Y are constants. Verbally, the covariance between X and Y is the expected value of the product of the two variables minus the product of the expected values of the two variables.

3.19. $\text{var}(aX) = E[aX - E(aX)]^2 = E\{a[X-E(X)]\}^2$
$$= a^2 E[X - E(X)]^2 = a^2 \text{var}(X).$$

3.20. $\text{var}(aX + bY) = E[(aX+bY) - E(aX+bY)]^2$
$$= E[aX - aE(X) + bY - bE(Y)]^2$$
$$= a^2 E[X - E(X)]^2 + b^2 E[Y - E(Y)]^2 + 2ab\,\text{cov}(X,Y)$$
$$= a^2 \text{var}(X) + b^2 \text{var}(Y), \text{ since X and Y are independent.}$$

3.21. (a) $P[|X - \mu_X|] \leq 2.5\sigma_X = 1 - \dfrac{1}{2.5^2} = 0.84$ or 84%.

(b) $P[|X - \mu_X|] \leq 8\sigma_X = 1 - \dfrac{1}{8^2} = 0.9844$ or about 98.44%.

3.22. $E(X-k)^2 = E[X - E(X) + E(X) - k]^2 = E[X - E(X)]^2 + E[E(X) - k]^2$
$$+ 2E[X - E(X)][E(X) - k]$$
$$= \text{var}(X) + E[E(X) - k]^2$$

For this to be equal to var(X), k must be equal to $E(X)$. In other words, the variance of a random variable is least when it is measured around the mean, or expected, value of that variable.

3.23. $\text{var}(Y|X=2) = (0-1.875)^2(0.0833) + (1-1.875)^2(0.25) + (2-1.875)^2(0.4167)$
$$+ (3-1.875)^2(0.2083) + (4-1.875)^2(0.0417) = 0.9427$$

Note: $f(Y=0|X=2) = f(Y=0, X=2)/f(X=2) \approx 0.0833$, and similarly for the other conditional probabilities.

3.24. $f(X) = \dfrac{3}{8}(4X - 2X^2)$. Therefore,

$$E(X) = \dfrac{3}{8}\int_0^2 X(4X - 2X^2)dx = \dfrac{3}{8}\left[4\dfrac{X^3}{3} - \dfrac{X^4}{2}\right]_0^2 = 1$$

$\text{var}(X) = E(X^2) - [E(X)]^2$

$$E(X^2) = \dfrac{3}{8}\int_0^2 [X^2(4X - 2X^2)]dx = \dfrac{3}{8}\left[X^4 - \dfrac{2}{5}X^5\right]_0^2 = 1.2$$

$\text{var}(X) = 1.2 - 1 = 0.2$.

CHAPTER

4

SOME IMPORTANT PROBABILITY DISTRIBUTIONS

QUESTIONS

4.1 (*a*) The number of independent observations available to compute an estimate, e.g., the sample mean or the sample variance.

(*b*) The probability distribution of an estimator.

(*c*) The standard deviation of an estimator.

4.2. (*a*) *True*, $P(Z) > 1 = 0.5000 - 0.3413 = 0.1587 \approx 0.16$

(*b*) *True*, $P(1 \leq Z \leq 1.5) = 0.4332 - 0.3413 = 0.0919 \approx 0.09$

(*c*) *True*, $P(Z) > 2.5 = 0.5000 - 0.4938 = 0.0062$.

4.3. (*a*) $\bar{X} \sim (8, 16/n)$

(*b*) The variance of $\bar{X}$ depends on the sample size.

(*c*) Since $\bar{X} \sim N(8, 16/25)$, the probability that $Z \leq -2.5 = 0.0062$.

4.4. Although both are symmetrical, the *t* distribution is flatter than the normal distribution. But as the degrees of freedom increase, the *t* distribution approximates the normal distribution.

4.5. (*a*) 0.10;   (*b*) 0.10;   (*c*) 0.20;   (*d*) No.

4.6. *True*.

4.7. (*a*) About 0.005.

(*b*) $Z = \sqrt{[2(80)]} - \sqrt{[(100-1)]} = 12.65 - 9.95 = 2.7$. $P(Z > 2.7) = 0.0035$.

(*c*) From the χ^2 table, this probability is somewhere between 0.90 and 0.95. From the normal approximation, we obtain it as:

$Z = \sqrt{[2(80)]} - \sqrt{[(200-1)]} = -1.46$. The probability of obtaining a Z value of -1.46 or greater is about 0.93 ($0.4279 + 0.5000 \cong 0.93$). As these calculations show, as the sample size increases, the normal approximation becomes increasingly accurate.

4.8. In large samples, the distribution of the sample mean of a r.v. can be approximated by a normal distribution regardless of the original population (i.e., PDF) from which the sample was drawn.

4.9. The chi-square distribution can be used to determine the probabilities for the sampling distribution of the sample variance S^2. In other words, a probability statement about a chi-square variable can be easily expressed into an equivalent probability statement about S^2. The F distribution can be used to find out if the variances of two normal populations are the same.

PROBLEMS

4.10. (*a*) $Z = (1 - 1.5) / 0.12 \cong -4.17$. The probability of obtaining a Z value equal to or less than -4.17 is extremely small.

(*b*) $Z_1 = (0.8 - 1.5) / 0.12 = -5.8333$; $Z_2 = (1.3 - 1.5) / 0.12 = -1.6667$. Therefore, $P(-5.8333 \leq Z \leq -1.6667)$ is very small. Note that the probability that (mean $\pm$ 1.96σ) = 0.95 is true for a normally distributed random variable. Given the mean of $1.5 million and σ of $0.12 million, the probability that a profit figure will be between 1.26 and 1.74 million is about 95%. Therefore, the probability that the profits will be between $0.8 and $1.3 million must be small indeed.

4.11. Since $P(Z \geq 1.28)$ is about 0.10, we obtain $1.28 = (X - 1.5) / 0.12$, which gives $X = \$1.6536$ million as the required figure.

4.12. From the preceding exercise, we know that $P(Z \geq 1.28) = 0.10$. Therefore, $1.28 = (80 - 75) / \sigma$, which gives $\sigma = 3.9063$.

4.13. (*a*) $Z = (6 - 6.5) / 0.8 = -0.625 \cong -0.63$. Therefore, $P(Z \leq -0.63) = 0.2643$. Thus, approximately, 264 tubes will contain less than 6 ounces of toothpaste.

(*b*) The cost of the refill will be $52.8 (= \$0.20 \times 264)$.

(*c*) $Z = (7 - 6.5) / 0.8 = 0.625 \cong 0.63$. The probability of $Z \geq 0.63$ is also $\cong 0.2643$. Therefore, the profits lost will be $13.2 (= \$0.05 \times 264)$.

4.14. (*a*) $(X + Y) \sim N(25, 11)$, (*b*) $(X - Y) \sim N(-5, 11)$,

(c) $3X \sim N(30, 27)$, (d) $(4X + 5Y) \sim N(115, 248)$.

4.15. In answering this question, note that if $W = (aX + bY)$,

$E(W) = a\mu_x + b\mu_y$

$\text{var}(W) = a^2 \text{var}(X) + b^2 \text{var}(Y) + 2ab\rho\sigma_x\sigma_y$ (see footnote 3, p. 80 of text)

(a) $(X + Y) \sim N(25, 16.88)$. (Note: $\sigma_x = 1.73$ and $\sigma_y = 2.83$)

(b) $(X - Y) \sim N(-5, 5.12)$

(c) $3X \sim N(30, 27)$

(d) $(4X + 5Y) \sim N(115, 365.58)$, approximately.

4.16. Let $W = 1/2(X) + 1/2(Y)$. In this example,

$E(W) = 1/2(15) + 1/2(8) = 11.5$

$\text{var}(W) = (1/4)(25) + (1/4)(4) + 2(1/2)(1/2)(-0.4)(5)(2) = 5.25$.

Therefore, $W \sim N(11.5, 5.25)$. The variance, hence the risk, of this portfolio is smaller than that of security X but greater than that of security Y. It is true that if you invest in security X, the expected return is higher than the portfolio return, but so is the risk. On the other hand, if you invest in security Y, the risk is smaller than that of the portfolio but so is the rate of return. Of course, you do not have to invest equally in the two securities.

4.17. If it is assumed that the SAT scores are normally distributed with mean and variance given in Example 4.12, it can be shown that:

$(n-1)(S^2/\sigma^2) \sim \chi^2_{(n-1)}$. In the present example, we have:

$\chi^2 = 9(85.21/83.88) = 9.14$, which is a chi-square variable with 9 d.f. From the χ^2 table, the probability of obtaining a chi-square of as much as 9.14 or greater is somewhere between 25% and 50%; the exact p value being 42.45%.

4.18. (a) We want $P[(S^2/\sigma^2) > X] = 0.10$. That is,

$P[(n-1)S^2/\sigma^2 > (n-1)X] = 0.10$. From the χ^2 table, we find that for 9 d.f., $9X = 14.6837$ or $X = 1.6315$. That is, the probability is 10 percent that S^2 will be more than 63% of the population variance.

(b) Following the same logic, it can be seen that:

$P[(n-1)X \leq (n-1)S^2/\sigma^2 \leq (n-1)Y] = 0.95$

Using the χ^2 table, we find the X and Y values as 0.3000 and 2.1136, respectively. (Note: For 9 d.f., $P(\chi^2 > 2.70039) = 0.975$ and $P(\chi^2 > 19.0228 = 0.025)$.

4.19. (*a*) Mean = 15.9880 ounces; variance = 0.0158 (ounces squared), standard deviation = 0.1257.

(*b*) $t = [(15.988 - 16) / (0.1257 / \sqrt{10})] = -0.3019$.

For 9 d.f., the probability of obtaining a *t* value of -0.3019 or smaller is greater than 0.25 (one-tailed), the *p* value being 0.3848. The *t* distribution is used here because the true variance is unknown.

4.20. Use the *F* distribution. Assuming both samples are independent and come from the normal populations and that the two population variances are the same, it can be shown that:

$$F = \frac{S_1^2}{S_2^2} \sim F \text{ with } (m-1) \text{ and } (n-1) \text{ d.f.}$$

In this example, $F = \dfrac{9}{7.2} = 1.25$. The probability of obtaining an *F* value of 1.25 or greater is 0.2371.

4.21-4.23. These exercises should be assigned as class exercises. The samples drawn will obviously differ from student to student. The point to note is that the sample means obtained from non-normal populations tend to be normally distributed as the sample size increases.

4.24. Recall that the following relationship between the *F* and the chi-square distribution holds as the degrees of freedom in the denominator increases indefinitely:

$$m \cdot F_{(m,n)} = \chi_m^2$$

where *m* are numerator d.f. From the statistical tables, we find that, at the 5% level, $\chi^2_{(10)} = 18.3070$. Now at the 5% level, the *F* values for $F_{10,10}$, $F_{10,20}$, and $F_{10,60}$ are, 2.98, 2.35, and 1.99, respectively. If we multiply the preceding values by 10, we obtain, 29.8, 23.5, and 19.9, which shows that as the denominator d.f. increase, the approximation becomes more accurate.

4.25. $\bar{X} = \frac{1}{n}\sum_{1}^{n} X_i$. Therefore, $E(\bar{X}) = \frac{1}{n}[E(X_1) + E(X_2) + ... + E(X_n)]$

$$= \frac{1}{n}[\mu_X + \mu_X + ... + \mu_X] = \frac{1}{n}(n\mu_X) = \mu_X$$

$$\text{var}(\bar{X}) = \text{var}\left(\frac{X_1 + X_2 + ... + X_n}{n}\right)$$

$$= \frac{1}{n^2}[\text{var}(X_1) + \text{var}(X_2) + ... + \text{var}(X_n)]$$

$$= \frac{1}{n^2}(n\sigma_X^2) = \frac{\sigma_X^2}{n}, \text{ because } X_i \text{ are i.i.d.}$$

4.26. $E\left[\dfrac{X - \mu_X}{\sigma_X}\right] = \dfrac{1}{\sigma_X} E(X - \mu_X) = 0$, because σ_X is a constant and the fact that:

$$E(X - \mu_X) = E(X) - E(\mu_X) = \mu_X - \mu_X = 0$$
$$\text{var}(Z) = E[Z - E(Z)]^2 = E(Z^2), \text{ since } E(Z) = 0.$$

Now:

$$E(Z^2) = E\left(\frac{X - \mu_X}{\sigma_X}\right)^2 = \frac{1}{\sigma_X^2} E(X - \mu_X)^2 = \frac{1}{\sigma_X^2} \cdot \sigma_X^2 = 1$$

CHAPTER 5

STATISTICAL INFERENCE: ESTIMATION AND HYPOTHESIS TESTING

QUESTIONS

5.1. (*a*) A single numerical value of a (population) parameter is known as a point estimate. An interval estimate provides a range of values that will include the true parameter with a certain degree of confidence (i.e., probability). A point estimator is a formula or rule that tells how to obtain the point estimate.

(*b*) A null hypothesis is the maintained hypothesis which is tested against another hypothesis, called the alternative hypothesis.

(*c*) Type I error: The error of rejecting a hypothesis when it is true. A type II error is the error of accepting (i.e., not rejecting) a false hypothesis.

(*d*) The probability of committing a type I error is known as the level of significance (or the size of the test). One minus the probability of committing a type I error is called the confidence coefficient.

(*e*) The probability of accepting a false hypothesis is called a type II error and (1 − prob. of type II error), that is, the probability of not committing a type II error is called the power of the test.

5.2. (*a*) The two branches of classical statistics, estimation of parameters and testing hypothesis about parameters, constitute statistical inference.

(*b*) The probability distribution of an estimator.

(*c*) It is synonymous with a confidence interval.

(*d*) A statistic used to decide whether a null hypothesis is rejected or not.

(*e*) That value of the test statistic which demarcates the acceptance region from the rejection region.

(*f*) It is the probability of committing a type I error.

(*g*) The exact level of significance of a test statistic.

5.3. (a) If the average, or expected, value of an estimator coincides with the true value of the parameter, that estimator is known as an unbiased estimator.

(b) In a group of competing estimators of a parameter the one with the least variance is called a minimum variance estimator.

(c) In the class of unbiased estimators, the one with the least variance is called an efficient estimator.

(d) An estimator which is a linear function of the observations.

(e) An unbiased linear estimator with the least possible variance.

5.4. (a) *True.* In classical statistics the parameter is assumed to be some fixed number, although unknown.

(b) *False.* It is $E(\hat{\mu}_X) = \mu_X$, where $\hat{\mu}_X$ is an estimator.

(c) *True.*

(d) *False.* To be efficient, an estimator must be unbiased and it must have minimum variance.

(e) *False.* No probabilistic assumption is required for an estimator to be BLUE.

(f) *True.*

(g) *False.* A type I error is when we reject a true hypothesis.

(h) *False.* A type II error occurs when we do not reject a false hypothesis.

(i) *True.* This can be proved formally.

(j) *False,* generally. Only when the sample size increases indefinitely, the sample mean will be normally distributed. If, however, the sample is drawn from a normal population to begin with, the sample mean is distributed normally regardless of the sample size.

(k) *Uncertain.* The p value is the exact level of significance. If the chosen level of significance, say, $\alpha = 5\%$, coincides with the p value, the two will mean the same thing.

5.5. See Section 5.5.

5.6. Disagree. The answer depends on the level of significance (α), the probability of committing a type I error, that one is willing to accept. There is nothing sacrosanct about the 5% or 10% level of significance.

PROBLEMS

5.7. (*a*) ≈ 1.96   (*b*) ≈ 1.65   (*c*) ≈ 2.58   (*d*) ≈ 2.05.

5.8. (*a*) 3.182 (3 d.f.)   (*b*) 2.353 (3 d.f.)   (*c*) 3.012 (13 d.f.)
(*d*) 2.650 (13 d.f.)   (*e*) 2.0003 (59 d.f.)   (*f*) 1.972 (199 d.f.)

Note: These critical values have been obtained from electronic statistical tables.

5.9. (*a*) $P(-2 \leq Z \leq 2) = 0.9544$ (*b*) $P(Z \geq 2) = 0.0228$
(*c*) $P(Z \leq -2) = 0.0228$ (*d*) Yes ($Z = 40$, an extremely high value)

5.10. Note that $\bar{X} \sim N(1{,}000, \sigma^2/n = 10)$

(*a*) Practically zero, because $P(Z \leq -31.6228)$ is negligible.

(*b*) The 95% confidence interval is: $893.8019 \leq \mu_{\bar{X}} \leq 906.1981$ With 95% confidence we can say that the true mean is not equal to 1,000.

(*c*) Reject the null hypothesis. Use the normal distribution because the sample size is reasonably large.

5.11. (*a*) Note that $(6.5 - \mu)/\sigma = -1.65$ and $(6.8 - \mu)/\sigma = 1.28$.

Solving these two equations simultaneously, we obtain the two results $\mu = 6.6689$ and $\sigma = 0.1024$.

(*b*) $Z = (7 - 6.6689)/0.1024 = 3.2333$. Therefore, $P(Z \geq 3.2333)$ is very small, about 0.0006.

5.12. Note that $\bar{X} = 9$.

(*a*) If $X \sim N(5, 2)$, then $\bar{X} \sim N(5, 2/10)$. Therefore,
$$Z = (9 - 5)/0.4472 = 8.9445.$$

Therefore, $P(Z \geq 8.9445)$ is practically zero. Hence, we reject the null hypothesis that $\mu = 5$. Also, note that the 95% confidence interval for $\bar{X}$ is:

$$\left(5 \pm 1.96 \frac{1.4142}{\sqrt{10}}\right) = (4.1235, 5.8765).$$

This interval does not include $\bar{X} = 9$.

(*b*) Also reject the null hypothesis.

(*c*) The *p* value is extremely small.

5.13. Use the t distribution, since the true σ^2 is unknown. For 9 d.f., the 5% critical t value is 2.262. Therefore, the 95% CI is:
$$8 \pm 2.262(1.2649) = (5.1388, 10.8612)$$

5.14. (a) $\bar{X} \sim N(8, 36/25)$

(b) $Z = (7.5 - 8)/1.2 = -0.4167$. Therefore, $P(Z \leq -0.4167) = 0.3372$.

(c) The 95% CI for $\bar{X} = 8 \pm 1.96(1.2) = (5.6480, 10.3520)$.

Since this interval includes the value of 7.5, such a sample could have come from this population.

5.15. Using electronic statistical tables, it can be found that

(a) $p = 0.0492$ (b) $p = 0.0019$

(c) $p = 0.0814$ (d) $p = 0.9400$

5.16. The answer depends on the level of α, the probability of a type I error. The p value in this case is about 0.25 (actually, 0.2509). If α is fixed at 0.25, one could reject the relevant null hypothesis at this level of significance.

5.17. (a) $E(\hat{\mu}_1) = [E(X_1) + E(X_2) + E(X_3)]/3 = 3\mu/3 = \mu$.

Hence it is an unbiased estimator. Similarly, it can be shown that $\hat{\mu}_2$ is also unbiased.

(b) $\text{var}(\hat{\mu}_1) = 1/9[\text{var}(X_1) + \text{var}(X_2) + \text{var}(X_3)] = 3\sigma^2/9 = 0.330\sigma^2$.

$\text{var}(\hat{\mu}_2) = 7/18\ \sigma^2 = 0.389\sigma^2$. So, choose $\hat{\mu}_1$ over $\hat{\mu}_2$.

5.18. (a) $900{,}000 \pm 2.262(100{,}000/\sqrt{10})$, that is, $(828{,}469,\ 971{,}531)$

(b) The t distribution, since the true σ^2 is not known.

5.19. (a) $(19)(16)/32.8523 \leq \sigma^2 \leq (19)(16)/8.9065$, that is, $(9.2535, 34.1324)$

Note: For 19 d.f., $\chi^2_{0.025} = 32.8523$ and $\chi^2_{0.975} = 8.9065$.

(b) Since the preceding interval does not include $\sigma^2 = 8.2$, reject the null hypothesis.

5.20. (a) $F = \dfrac{S_1^2}{S_2^2} = \dfrac{0.3762}{0.3359} = 1.12$. The p value of obtaining an F value of 1.12 or greater is 0.4146. Therefore, one may not reject the null hypothesis that the two population variances are the same.

(b) The F test is used. The basic assumption is that the two populations are normal.

5.21. $E(X^*) = \dfrac{1}{n+1}[E(X_1) + E(X_2) + ... + E(X_n)]$

$= \dfrac{1}{n+1}(n \cdot \mu_X) = \dfrac{n}{n+1}\mu_X \neq \mu_X$

5.22. Follow the hint given in the problem.

CHAPTER 6

BASIC IDEAS OF LINEAR REGRESSION: THE TWO-VARIABLE MODEL

QUESTIONS

6.1. (*a*) It states how the population *mean* value of the dependent variable is related to one or more explanatory variables.

(*b*) It is the sample counterpart of the PRF.

(*c*) It tells how the individual Y are related to the explanatory variables and the stochastic error term, u, in the population as a whole.

(*d*) A model that is linear in the parameters, the Bs.

(*e*) It is a proxy for all omitted or neglected variables that affect the dependent variable Y. The individual influence of each of these variables is random and small so that on average their influence on Y is zero.

(*f*) It is the sample counterpart of the stochastic error term.

(*g*) The expected value of Y conditional upon a given value of X. It is obtained from the conditional (probability) distribution of Y, given X.

(*h*) The expected value of an r.v. regardless of the values taken by other random variables. It is obtained from the unconditional, or marginal, probability distributions of the relevant random variables.

(*i*) The B coefficients in a linear regression model are called regression coefficients or regression parameters.

(*j*) The bs, which tell how to compute the Bs, are called the estimators. Numerical values taken by the bs are known as estimates.

6.2. A stochastic SRF tells how Y_i in a randomly drawn sample from a Y population are related to the explanatory variables and the residuals e_i. A stochastic PRF tells how the individual Y_i are related to the explanatory variables and the stochastic error term u_i in the whole population.

6.3. The PRF is a theoretical, or idealized, model, just as the model of perfect competition is an idealized model. But such idealized models help us to see the essence of the problem.

6.4. (*a*) *False*. The residual e_i is an approximation (i.e., an estimator) of the true error term, u_i.

(*b*) *False*. It gives the *mean* value of the dependent variable, given the values of the explanatory variables.

(*c*) *False*. A linear regression model is *linear in the parameters* and not necessarily linear in the variables.

(*d*) *False*, generally. The cause and effect relationship between the *X*s and *Y* must be justified by theory.

(*e*) *False*, unless the "conditioned" and conditioning variables are independent.

(*f*) *False*. It is the other way around.

(*g*) *False*. It measures the change in the *mean* value of Y per unit change in X.

(*h*) *Uncertain*. There are many a phenomena which can be explained by the two-variable model. One example is the *Market Model* of portfolio theory which regresses the rate of return on a single security on the rate of return on a market index (e.g., S&P 500 stock index). The slope coefficient in this model, popularly known as the *beta coefficient*, is used extensively in portfolio analysis.

(*i*) *True*.

6.5. (*a*) b_1 is an estimator of B_1.

(*b*) b_2 is an estimator of B_2.

(*c*) e_i is an estimator of u_i.

We never observe B_1, B_2, and u. Once we have a specific sample, we can obtain their estimates via b_1, b_2 and e.

6.6. By simple algebra, we obtain:
$$X_t = 2.5 - 2.5Y_t$$

Sometimes Okun's model is run in this format, regressing percent growth in real output on the change in the unemployment rate.

6.7. (a) The answer will depend on how the various components of GDP (consumption expenditure, investment expenditure, government expenditure and expenditure on net exports) react to the higher interest rate. For instance, *ceteris paribus*, investment expenditure and the interest rate are inversely related.

(b) Positive. *Ceteris paribus*, the higher the interest rate is, the greater will be the incentive to save.

(c) Generally positive.

(d) Positive, to maintain at least the status quo.

(e) Probably positive.

(f) Probably negative; familiarity may breed contempt.

(g) Probably positive.

(h) Positive. Statistics is a major foundation of econometrics.

(i) Positive. As income increases, discretionary income is likely to increase, leading to an increased demand for more expensive cars. A large number of Japanese cars are expensive. In general, the income elasticity of demand for items like cars has been found to be not only positive but generally greater than 1.

PROBLEMS

6.8. (a) Yes (b) Yes (c) Yes (d) Yes (e) No (f) No.

6.9. (a) The conditional expected values are:

Value of X	$E(Y\|X)$	Value of X	$E(Y\|X)$
80	65	180	125
100	77	200	137
120	89	220	149
140	101	240	161
160	113	260	173

(b) and **(c)**. This is straightforward.

(d) The mean of Y increases with X. That may not be true of the individual Y values.

(e) PRF: $Y_i = B_1 + B_2 X_i + u_i$

SRF: $Y_i = b_1 + b_2 X_i + e_i$

(f) The scatter plot will show that the PRF is linear.

6.10. **(a)** This is straightforward.

(b) The relationship between the two is positive.

(c) SRF: $\hat{Y}_i = 24.4545 + 0.5091 X_i$

The raw data give: $\sum Y_i = 1{,}110$; $\sum X_i = 1{,}700$; $\sum x_i^2 = 33{,}000$;

$\sum x_i y_i = 16{,}800$, where the small letters denote deviations from the mean values.

(d) This is straightforward.

(e) The two are close, but obviously they are not identical.

6.11. **(a)** From the time subscript t, it seems that this is a time series regression.

(b) The regression line is linear with a negative slope.

(c) The average number of cups of coffee consumed per person per day if the price of coffee were zero. Economically speaking, this may or may not make sense.

(d) *Ceteris paribus*, the *mean* consumption of coffee per day goes down by about 1/2 cup a day as the price of coffee per pound increases by a $1.

(e) No. But with the confidence interval procedure discussed in the next chapter, it is possible to tell, in probabilistic terms, what the PRF may be.

(f) We have information on the slope coefficient, but not on X and Y. Therefore, we cannot compute the price elasticity coefficient from the given information.

6.12. **(a)** and **(b)**. The scattergram will show that the relationship between the S&P 500 index and the CPI is positive.

(c) $(\hat{S\&P})_t = -195.5149 + 3.8264 \, CPI_t$

These results show that on average S&P goes up by about 3.8 points per unit increase in the CPI. The constant term suggests that if the value of the CPI were zero, the mean value of S&P would be about -195.

Note: This example is further examined in problem 6.15.

(d) The positive slope may make economic sense, but the negative intercept value may not.

(e) Most probably it was due to the October 1987 stock market crash.

6.13. **(a)** The scattergram will show a positive relationship between the nominal interest rate and the inflation rate, as per economic theory (the so-called *Fisher effect*). Notice that there is an extreme observation, called an *outlier*, pertaining to Mexico.

(b) $\hat{Y}_i = 2.7131 + 1.2320 X_i$

(c) The value of the slope coefficient is expected to be 1, because, according to the Fisher equation, the following relationship holds true approximately: nominal interest rate = expected real interest rate + expected inflation rate. Thus, the intercept in the Fisher equation is the expected real rate of interest. In the present example, we cannot tell whether the Fisher equation holds because the inflation rate used is the actual inflation rate. In terms of the actual inflation rate, the nominal rate, on average, seems to increase more than one percent for a one percent increase in the (actual) inflation rate, for the slope coefficient is 1.2320. Applying the techniques discussed in the next chapter, this slope coefficient is statistically significantly greater than 1.

6.14. **(a)** This is straightforward.

(b) $\hat{NE}_{US} = -0.4945 + 1.1632\ RE_{US}$

(c) Positive.

(d) Yes.

(e) $\ln \hat{NE}_{US} = -0.2535 + 1.2326 \ln RE_{US}$

Yes, the results are qualitatively the same. But note that the slope coefficient in the double-log model represents the elasticity coefficient, whereas that in the linear model represents the absolute rate of change in the (mean) value of NE$_{US}$ for a unit change in RE$_{US}$. See Chapter 9 for the various functional forms.

6.15. (*a*) Repeating the five questions, we have:
- The scattergram is straightforward.
- As before, the relationship between the two is expected to be positive.
- The regression equation for the 1990-2001 period is:
$$(\hat{S\&P})_t = -3{,}152.7333 + 25.4198 \; CPI_t$$
- The positive slope makes economic sense but the intercept does not.
- The 1988 S&P decline is not applicable here.

(*b*) The results are in accord with prior expectations, although numerical values of the two period regression coefficients are vastly different.

(*c*) Combining the two data sets, we get the following results:
$$(\hat{S\&P})_t = -909.2380 + 10.9354 \; CPI_t$$

(*d*) Since the regression results of the two sub-periods are different (which can be proved using the dummy variable technique discussed in Chapter 10 or by the Chow test), the preceding regression results that are based on the pooled data are not meaningful.

6.16. (*a*) ASP = - 85,495.27 + 50,315.30 GPA

It seems GPA has a positive impact on ASP.

(*b*) ASP = - 150,778.01 + 349.47 GMAT

GMAT also seems to have a positive impact on ASP.

(*c*) ASP = 44,249.98 + 1.38 TUITION

Tuition also seems to have positive impact on ASP.

Top business schools generally have top teachers and researchers. This means that these schools have to pay higher salaries to attract quality faculty. In this sense high tuition may be a proxy for high quality education, which may result in higher ASP for graduates from such schools.

(*d*) ASP = 1,812.43 + 21,985.05 RATING

This positive relationship suggests that recruiter perception has a positive bearing on ASP.

Note: In the next chapter we will see if the regressions presented above are statistically significant.

6.17. (*a*) Given the formulation of Okun's law in Equation (6.22), the new variables based on the real GDP (RGDP) and the unemployment rate (UNRATE) data from Table 6-12 can be calculated as follows:

CHUNRATE = Change in UNRATE = UNRATE − UNRATE(-1)

PCTCRGDP = % Change in RGDP = [RGDP / RGDP(-1)]*100-100

Note: UNRATE − UNRATE(-1) means subtracting the previous period's unemployment rate from the current period's unemployment rate. For example, looking at the first two observations, UNRATE − UNRATE(-1) = 5.9 − 4.9, and so on. Similarly for RGDP and RGDP(-1), except in this case we divide by the previous period's observation.

The regression equation is:

$$\widehat{CHUNRATE} = 1.2532 - 0.3986 \text{ PCTCRGDP}$$

The slope coefficients in the two regressions are about the same. If you simplify (6.22), the result is: CHUNRATE = 1.00 − 0.40 PCTCRGDP.

Therefore, the intercepts in the two regressions are about the same. Perhaps Okun's law may have some universal validity.

(*b*) Reversing the roles of CHUNRATE and PCTCRGDP, we have:

$$\widehat{PCTCRGDP} = 3.1601 - 1.8439 \text{ CHUNRATE}$$

For a unit change in CHUNRATE, real GDP growth changes by about 1.84 percent in the opposite direction.

(*c*) If CHUNRATE in (*b*) is zero, real GDP growth is about 3.2% We may interpret this as the natural rate of growth in real GDP. In the original Okun model it was assumed to be about 2.5%, the growth rate then prevailing.

6.18. (*a*) Straightforward. Any minor differences may be solely due to rounding issues.

(*b*) For model (6.24), the output is as follows:

obs	Actual	Fitted	Residual	Residual Plot
1980	118.780	210.870	-92.0901	
1981	128.050	170.197	-42.1465	
1982	119.710	228.240	-108.530	
1983	160.410	286.440	-126.030	
1984	160.460	256.491	-96.0308	
1985	186.840	332.874	-146.034	
1986	236.340	420.278	-183.938	
1987	286.830	432.261	-145.431	
1988	265.790	374.021	-108.231	
1989	322.840	305.410	17.4304	
1990	334.590	331.482	3.10808	
1991	376.180	465.311	-89.1315	
1992	415.740	739.907	-324.167	
1993	451.410	847.476	-396.066	
1994	460.420	591.979	-131.559	
1995	541.720	457.457	84.2633	
1996	670.500	503.629	166.871	
1997	873.430	498.509	374.921	
1998	1085.50	526.298	559.202	
1999	1327.33	543.740	783.590	

For model (6.25) the output is:

obs	Actual	Fitted	Residual	Residual Plot
1980	118.780	103.981	14.7987	
1981	128.050	-70.7789	198.829	
1982	119.710	160.848	-41.1378	
1983	160.410	303.707	-143.297	
1984	160.460	237.825	-77.3655	
1985	186.840	383.459	-196.619	
1986	236.340	487.483	-251.143	
1987	286.830	498.579	-211.749	
1988	265.790	438.245	-172.455	
1989	322.840	339.075	-16.2355	
1990	334.590	381.379	-46.7885	
1991	376.180	526.319	-150.139	
1992	415.740	662.937	-247.197	
1993	451.410	692.757	-241.347	
1994	460.420	604.683	-144.263	
1995	541.720	520.077	21.6429	
1996	670.500	554.058	116.442	
1997	873.430	550.591	322.839	
1998	1085.50	568.622	516.878	
1999	1327.33	579.024	748.306	

The residual plots of the two models seem similar. To choose between the two models, we need model selection criteria, discussed in Chapter 11.

6.19. (*a*) The graphs are as follows:

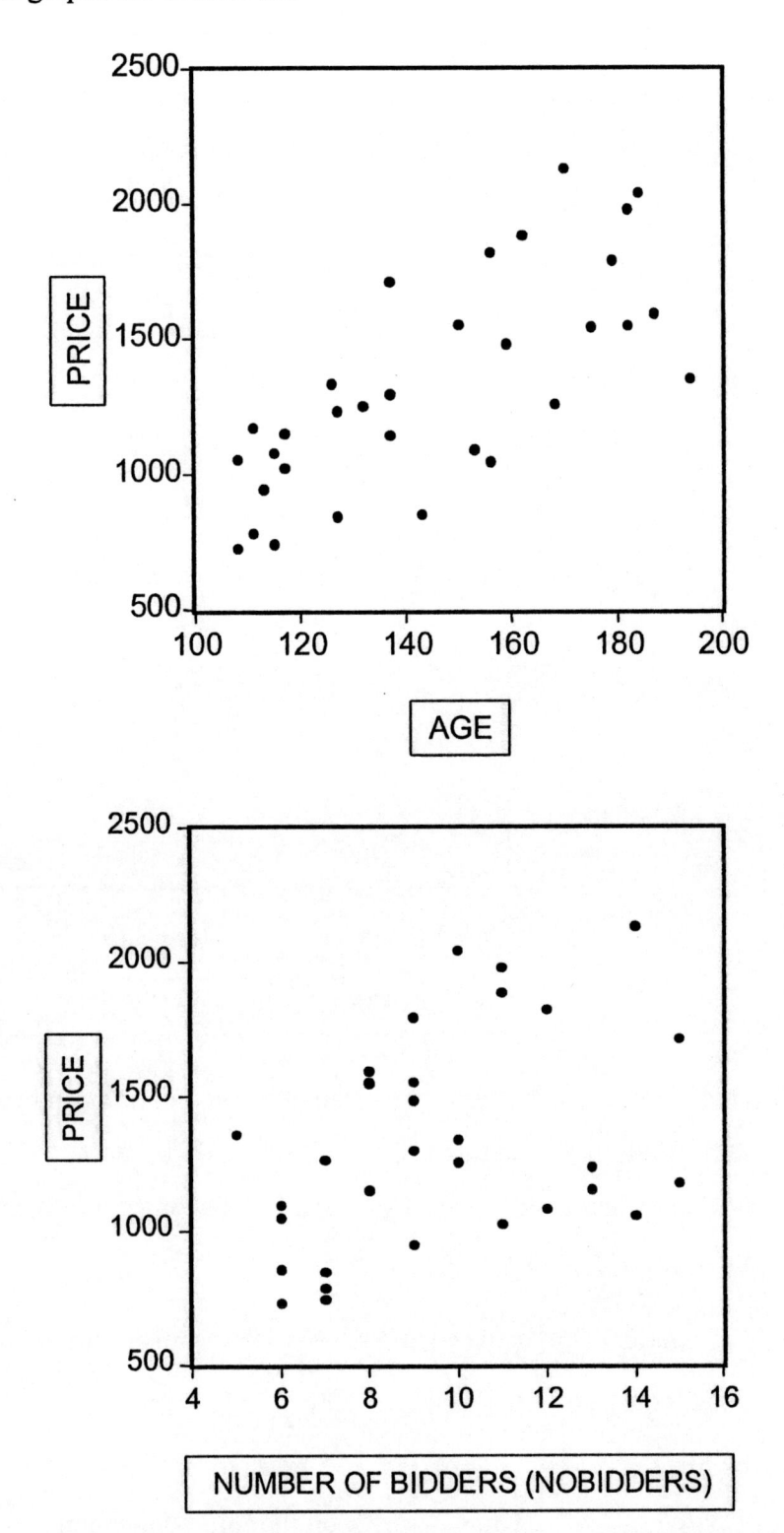

This graph shows that the higher the number of bidders, the higher the price is. This probably is true of the antique clock auction market. As a first approximation, the linear model may be appropriate for the price/age relationship, but may not be quite appropriate for the price/number of bidders relationship.

(**b**) The plot of the number of bidders versus age is as follows:

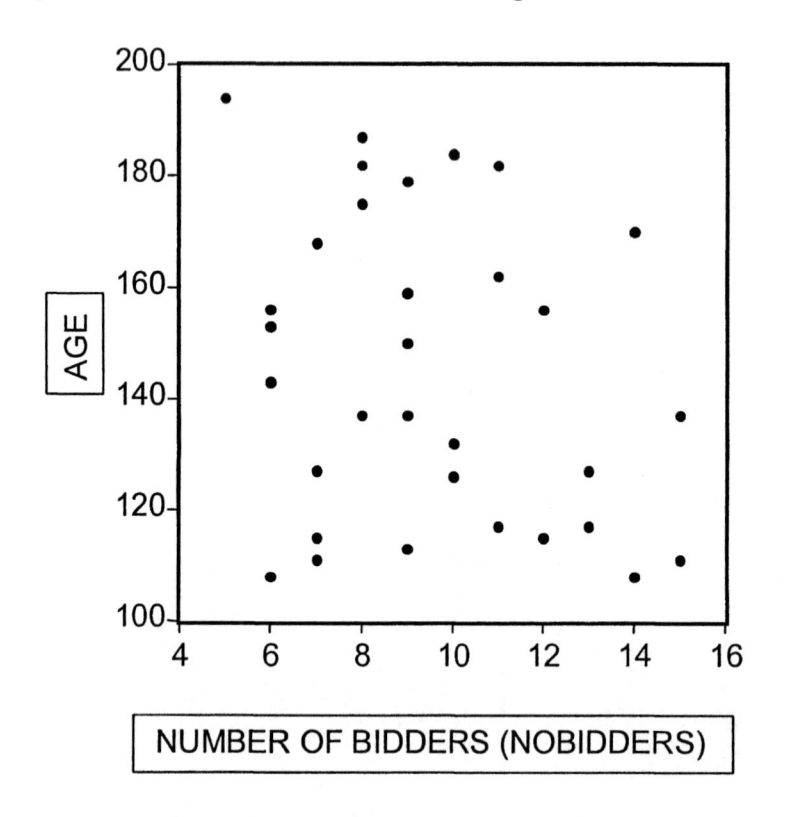

This scatter plot shows a very weak negative relationship between clock age and the number of bidders. This is most likely because, the higher the clock age, the higher the price. There will be fewer people able to bid for the older, more expensive clocks.

6.20. The scatter plot between actual Y (data from Table 6.4) and estimated $\hat{Y}$ values is as follows:

(Graph appears on the following page)

[Scatter plot of YHAT (ESTIMATED) vs Y (ACTUAL)]

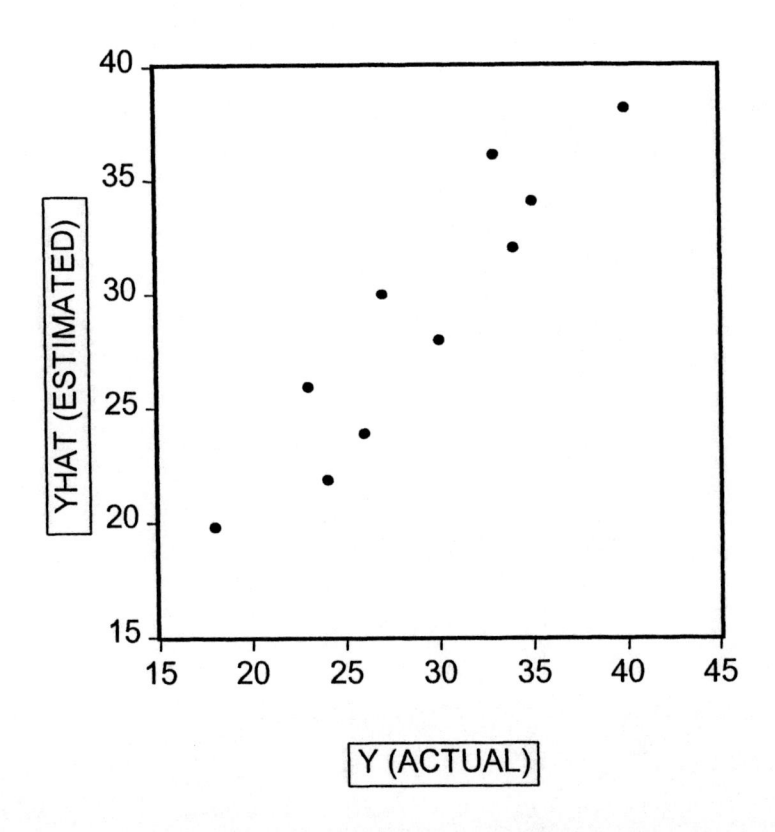

If the fitted model is a good one, the actual and estimated Y values should be very close to each other. In the case where the model is a perfect fit, the scatter points will lie on a straight line.

6.21. (*a*) MATHM = 262.7990 + 0.5385 VERBM

(*b*) This regression suggests that as the male verbal score goes up by a unit, on average, the male math score goes up by about 0.5 units.

(*c*) VERBM = -380.4789 + 1.6417 MATHM

As per this regression if the male math score goes up by a unit, the average male verbal score goes up by about 1.64 units.

(*d*) If you multiply the slope coefficients in the two preceding equations, you will obtain: (0.5385)(1.6417) = 0.8841

As we show in the next chapter, the r^2 value, which is a measure of how good a chosen regression line fits the actual data, for either of the preceding regressions is 0.8841, which is precisely equal to the product of the slope coefficients in the two preceding regressions. The point to note here is that in a bivariate regression, if we regress Y on X or vice versa, the r^2 value remains the same.

OPTIONAL QUESTIONS

6.22. $\sum e_i = \sum (Y_i - b_1 - b_2 X_i)$

$= n\bar{Y} - \sum(\bar{Y} - b_2\bar{X}) - b_2 \sum X_i$ [Note: $b_1 = \bar{Y} - b_2\bar{X}$]

$= n\bar{Y} - n\bar{Y} + b_2\, n\bar{X} - b_2\, n\bar{X} = 0$

6.23. $\sum e_i X_i = \sum (Y_i - b_1 - b_2 X_i) X_i$

$= \sum Y_i X_i - b_1 \sum X_i - b_2 \sum X_i^2$

$= 0$, because of Equation (6.15).

6.24. $\sum e_i \hat{Y}_i = \sum e_i (b_1 + b_2 X_i)$

$= b_1 \sum e_i + b_2 \sum e_i X_i = 0$, using problems (6.22) and (6.23) above.

6.25. Since $Y_i = \hat{Y}_i + e_i$, summing over both sides over the sample, we obtain:

$$\sum Y_i = \sum \hat{Y}_i + \sum e_i$$

Dividing both sides by n, we obtain:

$$\sum Y_i / n = \sum \hat{Y}_i / n + \sum e_i / n$$

Since the last term in this equation is zero (why?), the result follows.

6.26. $\sum x_i y_i = \sum x_i (Y_i - \bar{Y}) = \sum x_i Y_i - \bar{Y} \sum x_i = \sum x_i Y_i$, since $\bar{Y}$ is a constant and since $\sum x_i = \sum(X_i - \bar{X}) = 0$, as shown in Equation (6.17). The other expressions in this problem can be derived similarly.

6.27. $\sum x_i = \sum(X_i - \bar{X}) = \sum X_i - n\bar{X}$, since $\bar{X}$ is a constant

$= n\bar{X} - n\bar{X} = 0$ since $\bar{X} = \sum X_i / n$

A similar result hold for $\sum y_i$.

It is worth remembering that the sum of deviations of a random variable from its mean value is always zero.

6.28. It is a simple matter of verification, save the rounding errors.

CHAPTER 7

THE TWO-VARIABLE REGRESSION MODEL: HYPOTHESIS TESTING

QUESTIONS

7.1. (*a*) In the regression context, the method of least squares estimates the regression parameters in such a way that the sum of the squared difference between the actual *Y* values (i.e., the values of the dependent variable) and the estimated *Y* values is as small as possible.

(*b*) The estimators of the regression parameters obtained by the method of least squares.

(*c*) An estimator being a random variable, its variance, like the variance of any random variable, measures the spread of the estimated values around the mean value of the estimator.

(*d*) The (positive) square root value of the variance of an estimator.

(*e*) Equal variance.

(*f*) Unequal variance.

(*g*) Correlation between successive values of a random variable.

(*h*) In the regression context, TSS is the sum of squared difference between the individual and the mean value of the dependent variable *Y*, namely, $\sum (Y_i - \bar{Y})^2$.

(*i*) ESS is the part of the TSS that is explained by the explanatory variable(s).

(*j*) RSS is the part of the TSS that is not explained by the explanatory variable(s), the *X* variable(s).

(*k*) It measures the proportion of the total variation in *Y* explained by the explanatory variables. In short, it is the ratio of ESS to TSS.

(*l*) It is the standard deviation of the *Y* values about the estimated regression line.

(*m*) BLUE means best linear unbiased estimator, that is, a linear estimator that is unbiased and has the least variance in the class of all such linear unbiased estimators.

(*n*) A statistical procedure of testing statistical hypotheses.

(*o*) A test of significance based on the *t* distribution.

(*p*) In a one-tailed test, the alternative hypothesis is one-sided. For example: $H_0 : \mu = \mu_0$ against $H_1 : \mu > \mu_0$ or $\mu < \mu_0$, where μ is the mean value.

(*q*) In a two-tailed test, the alternative hypothesis is two-sided.

(*r*) It is a short-hand for the statement: reject the null hypothesis.

7.2. (*a*) *False*. It minimizes the sum of residuals squared, that is, it minimizes $\sum e_i^2$.

(*b*) *True*.

(*c*) *True*.

(*d*) *False*. The OLS does not require any probabilistic assumption about the error term in estimating the parameters.

(*e*) *True*. The OLS estimators are linear functions of u_i and will follow the normal distribution if it is assumed that u_i are normally distributed. Recall that any linear function of a normally distributed variable is itself normally distributed.

(*f*) *False*. It is ESS / TSS.

(*g*) *False*. We should reject the null hypothesis.

(*h*) *True*. The numerator of both coefficients involves the covariance between *Y* and *X*, which can be positive or negative.

(*i*) *Uncertain*. The *p value* is the exact level of significance of a computed test statistic, which may be different from an arbitrarily chosen level of significance, α.

7.3. (*a*) t (*b*) se(b_2) (*c*) 0 and 1 (*d*) -1 and +1

(*e*) ESS (*f*) ESS (*g*) the standard error of the estimate

(*h*) $\sum (Y_i - \bar{Y})^2$ (*i*) $b_2^2 \sum x_i^2 + \sum e_i^2$

7.4. The answers to the missing numbers are in boxes:

$$\hat{Y}_i = -66.1058 + 0.0650\, X_i \qquad r^2 = 0.9460$$

$$\text{se} = (10.7509) \quad (\boxed{0.0035}) \qquad n = 20$$

$$t = (\boxed{-6.1489}) \quad (18.73)$$

The critical t value at the 5% level for 18 d.f. is 2.101 (two-tailed) and 1.734 (one-tailed). Since the estimated t value of 18.73 far exceeds either of these critical values, we reject the null hypothesis. A two-tailed test is appropriate because no *a priori* theoretical considerations are known regarding the sign of the coefficient.

7.5. $r^2 = (\sum y_i^2 - \sum e_i^2)/\sum y_i^2$

$\qquad = \sum \hat{y}_i^2 / \sum y_i^2$

$\qquad = b_2^2 \sum x_i^2 / \sum y_i^2$, following Equations (7.34) and (7.35)

In proving the last equality, note that $\sum y_i \hat{y}_i = b_2 \sum y_i x_i$. Then the result follows by substitution.

7.6. $\sum e_i = n\bar{Y} - n(\bar{Y} - b_2 \bar{X}) - n b_2 \bar{X} = 0$. See also Problem 6.22.

PROBLEMS

7.7. (a) The d.f. here are 14. Therefore, the 5% critical t value is 2.145. So, the 95% confidence interval is:

$$3.24 \pm 2.145(1.634) = (-0.2649, 6.7449)$$

(b) The preceding interval does include B_2. Therefore, do not reject the null hypothesis.

(c) $t = 3.24 / 1.634 = 1.9829$. Since car sales are expected to be positively related to real disposable income, the null and alternative hypotheses should be: $H_0 : B_2 \leq 0$ and $H_1 : B_2 > 0$. Therefore, an one-tailed t test is appropriate in this case. The 5% one-tailed t value for 14 d.f. is 1.761. Since the computed t value of 1.9829 exceeds the critical value, reject the null hypothesis (one- and two tail tests sometimes give different results).

7.8. **(a)** The slope coefficient of 1.0598 means that during the 1956–1976 period a percentage point increase in the market rate of return lead to about 1.06 percent points increase in the mean return on the IBM stock. In the same period, if the market rate of return were zero, the average rate of return on the stock would have been about 0.73 percent, which may not make economic sense.

(b) About 47 percent of the variation in the mean return on the IBM stock was explained by the (variation) in the market return.

(c) $H_0 : B_2 \leq 1$, $H_1 : B_2 > 1$. Hence:

$$t = \frac{(1.0598 - 1)}{0.0728} = 0.8214.$$

For 238 d.f, this t value is not statistically significant at the 5% level on the basis of the one-tailed t test. Thus, during the study period, the *beta coefficient* of IBM was not statistically different from unity, suggesting that the IBM stock was not volatile or aggressive.

7.9. **(a)** $b_1 = 21.22$; $b_2 = 0.5344$

(b) se(b_1) = 8.5894; se(b_2) = 0.0484

(c) $r^2 = 0.9385$

(d) 95% CI for B_1: 1.4128 to 41.0272

95% CI for B_2: 0.4228 to 0.6460

(e) Reject H_0, since the preceding CI does not include $B_2 = 0$.

7.10. **(a)** The answers to the missing numbers are in boxes:

$$\widehat{GNP}_t = -787.4723 + 8.0863\, M_{1t} \qquad r^2 = 0.9912$$

$$\text{se} = (\boxed{77.9675}) \quad (0.2197)$$

$$t = (-10.10001)\,(\boxed{36.8061})$$

(b) $H_0 : B_2 \leq 0$, $H_1 : B_2 > 0$. The null hypothesis can be rejected.

(c) No particular economic meaning can be attached to it.

(d) $\widehat{GNP}_{1984} = -787.4723 + 8.0863\,(552) \approx 3{,}676$ billion.

7.11. (*a*) Negative.

(*b*) Yes. Here, $n = 14$ (14 presidential elections starting in 1928 and ending in 1980) and therefore d.f. = 12. The computed t value of -2.67 is statistically significant at the five percent level (one-tailed test).

(*c*) Probably. But in the 1984 elections the personal popularity of Ronald Reagan was an important factor.

(*d*) Since $t = b_i / se(b_i)$ under the null hypothesis that the true B_i is zero, $se(b_i) = \dfrac{b_i}{t}$. In the present example these standard errors are 1.5572 and 0.6367, respectively.

7.12. (*a*) It could be negative or positive. As more output is produced as a result of increased capacity, price increases (i.e., inflation) will slow down. However, if capacity utilization is at its optimal value, and if demand pressures continue, inflation may actually rise.

(*b*) The output in *EViews* format is as follows:

Dependent Variable: INFLATION				
Sample: 1970 2001				
Variable	Coefficient	Std. Error	t-Statistic	Prob.
C	11.68771	10.22329	1.143243	0.2620
CAPACITY	-0.090540	0.127270	-0.711399	0.4823
R-squared	0.016590			

(*c*) The estimated slope coefficient is negative but also statistically insignificant, for the estimated p value is quite high.

(*d*) Yes it is, for under the null hypothesis that the true slope coefficient is 1, the estimated t value is

$$t = \frac{-0.0905 - (1)}{0.1272} = -8.5731$$

The probability of obtaining such a t value is practically zero.

(*e*) To get this, solve $11.6877 - 0.0905C = 0$, which gives $C \approx 129.14$, which may be called the "natural" rate of capacity utilization.

Note: The results of the above regression are virtually insignificant. Plus, the "natural" rate of capacity utilization that was found to be 129.14 may be problematic because the measure of capacity utilization does not exceed 100. The reason for the regression breakdown is the fact that the data include the decade of the 1970s with its high rates of inflation and the mid 1970s stagflation. Running the regression over a period that excludes the 1970s, say 1982-2001, will produce more reasonable and statistically significant results. In fact, if the regression covers the 1982-2001 period, the reader can easily verify that the "natural" rate of capacity utilization is approximately 93.90.

7.13. (*a*) The *EViews* regression results are as follows:

Dependent Variable: CAPACITY Sample: 1970 2001				
Variable	Coefficient	Std. Error	t-Statistic	Prob.
C	81.06023	1.305610	62.08610	0.0000
INFLATION	-0.183231	0.257565	-0.711399	0.4823
R-squared	0.016590			

Note: This regression is also insignificant for the reason discussed above.

(*b*) Multiplying the two slope coefficients, we obtain the value of 0.01659 which is equal to the R^2 value obtained from either equation. This result is not surprising in view of Problem 6.21.

(*c*) By way of another example, let Y = salary and X = qualifications for a group of men and women. As Maddala notes, the direct regression will answer the question whether men and women with the same X value get the same Y value. The reverse regression will answer the questions whether men and women with the same Y value will have the same X value. Reverse regression is advocated for wage discrimination cases.

(*d*) No.

7.14. (*a*) Positive.

(*b*) and (*c*) The scattergram will show that the relationship between the two is generally positive, although there are a few outliers.

(d) The regression results are as follows:

$$\hat{Y}_t = 373.3014 + 0.4199 X_t$$

$$\text{se} = (9530.3786) \quad (0.1154)$$

$$t = (0.0392) \quad (3.6406) \quad r^2 = 0.5464$$

(e) 99% CI: $0.0615 \le B_2 \le 0.7783$.

Since the preceding interval does not include zero, we can reject the null hypothesis.

7.15. (a) The regression results are:

$$\widehat{\text{MATHM}}_t = 175.9748 + 0.7142 \text{ MATHFM}_t$$

$$\text{se} = (20.6353) \quad (0.0455)$$

$$t = (8.5279) \quad (15.7056) \quad r^2 = 0.9181$$

(b) Reject the null hypothesis, since the computed t value of 15.7056 far exceeds the critical value even at the 0.001 level of significance.

(c) $\widehat{\text{MATHM}}_{1991} = 504.523 \approx 505$

(d) CI: (503.4877, 505.5583)

7.16. (a) The regression results are as follows:

$$\widehat{\text{VERBM}}_t = 148.1348 + 0.6727 \text{ VERBFM}_t$$

$$\text{se} = (11.6528) \quad (0.0268)$$

$$t = (12.7123) \quad (25.1018) \quad r^2 = 0.9663$$

(b) Reject the null hypothesis, since the computed t value is very high.

(c) $\widehat{\text{VERBM}}_{1991} \approx 434$

(d) CI: (432.9151, 435.0849)

7.17. (a) There is a positive relationship between real return on the stock price index this year and the dividend price ratio last year: Per unit increase in the latter, the mean real return goes up by 5.26 percentage points. The intercept has no viable economic meaning.

(b) If the preceding results are accepted, it has serious implications for the efficient market hypothesis of modern finance.

7.18 (*a*) The *EViews* regression output is as follows:

Dependent Variable: AVGHWAGE				
Sample: 1 13				
Variable	Coefficient	Std. Error	t-Statistic	Prob.
C	-0.014453	0.874624	-0.016525	0.9871
YEARSSCH	0.724097	0.069581	10.40648	0.0000
R-squared	0.907791			

(*b*) On the basis of the *t* test this hypothesis can be easily rejected, for the computed *t* value is highly significant; its *p* value is practically zero.

(*c*) Here $t = \dfrac{0.7240 - 1}{0.0695} = -3.9712$. This *t* value is also highly significant, leading to the conclusion that the education coefficient is statistically different from 1. The *p* value of obtaining the computed *t* value is 0.0011 (two-tail test).

7.19. *Note*: This Problem is an extension of Problem 6.17.

(*a*) Based on the regression, we need to calculate new variables based on the real GDP (RGDP) and the unemployment rate (UNRATE). These calculations, based on the data in Table 6-12, are as follows:

CHUNRATE = Change in UNRATE = UNRATE – UNRATE(-1)

PCTCRGDP = % Change in RGDP = [RGDP / RGDP(-1)]*100-100

Using *EViews*, the regression results are:

Dependent Variable: PCTCRGDP				
Sample (adjusted): 1971 1999				
Variable	Coefficient	Std. Error	t-Statistic	Prob.
C	3.160132	0.211050	14.97338	0.0000
CHUNRATE	-1.843945	0.213080	-8.653755	0.0000
R-squared	0.735002			

Note: The sample is adjusted to start in 1971 instead of the initial observation of 1970 because we are calculating percentage changes (RGDP) and changes (UNRATE): This causes the loss of the first observation.

(b) Yes, for the estimated slope coefficient has a *t* value of -8.6537 whose *p* value is practically zero.

(c) The intercept term is also statistically significant. The interpretation here is that if the change in the unemployment rate were zero, the growth in the real GDP will be about 3.2%, which may be called the long-term, or steady-state, rate of growth of GDP.

7.20. The regression results, using *EViews*, are:

| Dependent Variable: SP500 |||||
| Sample: 1980 1999 |||||
Variable	Coefficient	Std. Error	t-Statistic	Prob.
C	-15.57848	181.5552	-0.085806	0.9326
1/MTB3	2606.424	1000.085	2.606203	0.0179
R-squared	0.273968			

As these results show, the slope coefficient is statistically significant at about the 2% level, but the intercept is not. Any minor differences with the regression shown in the text are solely due to rounding.

7.21. The *EViews* regression results for (6.27) are as follows:

| Dependent Variable: PRICE |||||
| Sample: 1 32 |||||
Variable	Coefficient	Std. Error	t-Statistic	Prob.
C	-191.6662	264.4393	-0.724802	0.4742
AGE	10.48562	1.793729	5.845711	0.0000
R-squared	0.532509			

The estimated slope coefficient is highly statistically significant, for the *p* value of obtaining a *t* statistic of 5.8457 or greater under the null hypothesis of a zero true population slope coefficient is practically zero. In contrast, the estimated intercept coefficient is statistically insignificant since its *p* value is relatively high.

Likewise, the *EViews* results of regression (6.28) are:

(Regression output is shown in the following page)

Dependent Variable: PRICE				
Sample: 1 32				
Variable	Coefficient	Std. Error	t-Statistic	Prob.
C	807.9501	231.0921	3.496226	0.0015
NOBIDDERS	54.57245	23.26605	2.345582	0.0258
R-squared	0.154971			

Here both the coefficients are individually statistically significant, as their p values are quite low.

7.22. *Note*: The regression results presented here are identical to those of Problem 6.16.

(a) The results, using *EViews*, are as follows:

Dependent Variable: ASP				
Sample: 1 47				
Variable	Coefficient	Std. Error	t-Statistic	Prob.
C	-85495.27	47723.75	-1.791462	0.0799
GPA	50315.30	14156.75	3.554157	0.0009
R-squared	0.219184			

As these results suggest, GPA has a positive impact on ASP, and it is statistically very significant, as the p value of the estimated coefficient is very small.

(b) The results for GMAT are as follows:

Dependent Variable: ASP				
Sample: 1 47				
Variable	Coefficient	Std. Error	t-Statistic	Prob.
C	-150778.0	29251.36	-5.154565	0.0000
GMAT	349.4735	43.50542	8.032873	0.0000
R-squared	0.589143			

These results show that GMAT has a positive and statistically significant impact on ASP.

(c) The results for annual tuition are as follows:

(Regression output is shown in the following page)

Dependent Variable: ASP				
Sample: 1 47				
Variable	Coefficient	Std. Error	t-Statistic	Prob.
C	44249.98	5645.581	7.837985	0.0000
TUITION	1.381765	0.192217	7.188560	0.0000
R-squared	0.534525			

Tuition (perhaps reflecting the quality of education) has a positive and statistically significant impact on ASP.

Incidentally, it can also be shown that the impact of recruiter rating has a positive and highly significant impact on ASP, as it can be seen from the following *EViews* output:

Dependent Variable: ASP				
Sample: 1 47				
Variable	Coefficient	Std. Error	t-Statistic	Prob.
C	1812.437	6440.176	0.281427	0.7797
RATING	21985.05	1710.045	12.85642	0.0000
R-squared	0.786007			

7.23. The regression results of expenditure on imported goods (Y) and personal disposable income (X), using *EViews*, are as follows:

Dependent Variable: Y				
Sample: 1968 1987				
Variable	Coefficient	Std. Error	t-Statistic	Prob.
C	-260.7708	32.06653	-8.132180	0.0000
X	0.245652	0.015144	16.22099	0.0000
R-squared	0.935971			

These results suggest that personal disposable income has a very significant positive impact on expenditure on imported goods, an unsurprising finding. The p value for the slope is virtually zero, and the null hypothesis is therefore rejected.

7.24. If we let $w_i = \dfrac{x_i}{\sum x_i^2}$, we can write $b_2 = \sum w_i Y_i$, that is, b_2 is a linear estimator, i.e., a linear function of the Y values. Note that we are treating

X as non-stochastic. Follow similar steps to show that b_1 is also a linear function of the Y values.

Now:

$$b_2 = \frac{\sum x_i y_i}{\sum x_i^2} = \frac{\sum x_i Y_i}{\sum x_i^2} = \frac{\sum x_i (B_1 + B_2 X_i + u_i)}{\sum x_i^2}$$

$$= B_1 \frac{\sum x_i}{\sum x_i^2} + B_2 \frac{\sum x_i X_i}{\sum x_i^2} + \frac{\sum x_i u_i}{\sum x_i^2}$$

$$= B_2 + \frac{\sum x_i u_i}{\sum x_i^2}$$

This is in view of the fact that $\sum x_i = \sum (X_i - \bar{X}) = 0$ and $\frac{\sum x_i X_i}{\sum x_i^2} = 1$.

Therefore, $E(b_2) = E\left[B_2 + \frac{\sum x_i u_i}{\sum x_i^2}\right] = B_2$

Note: $E\left(\frac{\sum x_i u_i}{\sum x_i^2}\right) = \frac{1}{\sum x_i^2} E(\sum x_i u_i)$, since $\sum x_i^2$ is a constant and since X and u are uncorrelated by OLS assumption. Follow similar steps to prove that b_1 is also unbiased.

7.25. Squaring Equation (7.33) and summing, we obtain:

$$\sum y_i^2 = b_2^2 \sum x_i^2 + \sum e_i^2 + 2b_2 \sum x_i e_i$$
$$= b_2^2 \sum x_i^2 + \sum e_i^2$$

since $\sum x_i e_i = 0$.

CHAPTER 8

MULTIPLE REGRESSION: ESTIMATION AND HYPOTHESIS TESTING

QUESTIONS

8.1. (*a*) It measures the change in the *mean* value of the dependent variable (Y) for a unit change in the value of an explanatory variable (X), holding the values of all other explanatory variables constant. Mathematically, it is the partial derivative of (mean) Y with respect to the given explanatory variable.

(*b*) It measures the proportion, or percentage, of the total variation in the dependent variable, $\sum(Y_i - \bar{Y})^2$, explained by *all* the explanatory variables included in the model.

(*c*) Exact *linear* relationship among the explanatory variables.

(*d*) More than one exact *linear* relationship among the explanatory variables.

(*e*) Testing the hypothesis about a single (partial) regression coefficient.

(*f*) Testing the hypothesis about two or more partial regression coefficients simultaneously.

(*g*) An R^2 value that is adjusted for degrees of freedom.

8.2. (*a*) (1) State the null and alternative hypotheses.

(2) Choose the level of significance.

(3) Find the *t* value of the coefficient under the null hypothesis, H_0.

(4) Compare this $|t|$ value with the critical value at the chosen level of significance and the given d.f.

(5) If the computed *t* value exceeds the critical *t* value, we reject the null hypothesis. Make sure that you use the appropriate one-tailed or two-tailed test.

(*b*) Here the null hypothesis is:

$$H_0 : B_2 = B_3 = ... = B_k = 0$$

that is, all partial slopes are zero. The alternative hypothesis is that this is not so, that is, one or more partial slope coefficients are nonzero. Here, we use the ANOVA technique and the F test. If the computed F value under the null hypothesis exceeds the critical F value at the chosen level of significance, we reject the null hypothesis. Otherwise, we do not reject it. Make sure that the numerator and denominator d.f. are properly counted.

Note: In both (*a*) and (*b*), instead of choosing the level of significance in advance, obtain the *p* value of the estimated test statistic. If it is reasonably low, you can reject the null hypothesis.

8.3. (*a*) *True*. This is obvious from the formula relating the two R^2s.

(*b*) *False*. Use the F test.

(*c*) *False*. When $R^2 = 1$, the value of F is infinite. But when it is zero, the F value is also zero.

(*d*) *True*, which can be seen from the normal and *t* distribution tables.

(*e*) *True*. It can be shown that $E(b_{12}) = B_2 + B_3 b_{32}$, where b_{32} is the slope coefficient in the regression of X_3 on X_2. From this relationship, the conclusion follows.

(*f*) *False*. It is statistically different from zero, not 1.

(*g*) *False*. We also need to know the level of significance.

(*h*) *False*. By the overall significance we mean that all partial regression coefficients are not simultaneously equal to zero, or that R^2 is different from zero.

(*i*) *Partially true*. If our concern is only with a single regression coefficient, then we use the *t* test in both cases. But if we are interested in testing the joint significance of two or more partial regression coefficients, the *t* test will not do; we will have to use the F test.

(*j*) *True*. This is because TSS = $\sum(Y_i - \bar{Y})^2$. We lose only one d.f. in computing the sample mean. Therefore, the d.f. are always $(n-1)$.

8.4. (*a*) $\hat{\sigma}^2 = 880/21 = 41.9048$.

(*b*) $\hat{\sigma}^2 = 1220/10 = 122$.

8.5.   2.179;   2.528;   -1.697;   1.960 (normal approximation).

8.6.   5.05;   4.50;   1.62.

PROBLEMS

8.7. $\hat{Y}_i = -3.0 + 3.5 X_{2i}$

$\hat{Y}_i = 4.0 - 1.3571 X_{3i}$

$\hat{Y}_i = 2.0 + X_{2i} - X_{3i}$

(1) and **(2)** No, in both cases. As pointed out in Sec. 8.9, running a two-variable regression when a three-variable regression is called for is likely to give biased estimates of the true parameters. [See answer to question 8.3(e).] Only when $cov(X_2, X_3) = 0$ can one obtain unbiased estimates of the true parameters from the two-variable regressions. Even then, this procedure is not recommended because the standard errors can still be biased.

8.8.   **(a), (b),** and **(c)** $\hat{Y}_i = 53.1600 + 0.7266 X_{2i} + 2.7363 X_{3i}$

$\quad\quad$ se = (13.0261)   (0.0487)   (0.8486)

$\quad\quad$ t = (4.0810)   (14.9199)   (3.2245)

$\quad\quad\quad\quad\quad\quad\quad\quad\quad\quad\quad\quad R^2 = 0.9988; \ \bar{R}^2 = 0.9986$

(d) For 12 d.f. the two-tailed 5% critical t value is 2.179

95% CI for B_2: $0.7266 \pm 2.179 (0.0487)$ or $0.6205 \leq B_2 \leq 0.8327$

95% CI for B_3: $2.7363 \pm 2.179 (0.8486)$ or $0.8872 \leq B_3 \leq 4.5854$

(e) The null hypothesis that each partial slope coefficient is zero can be easily rejected at the 5% level of significance, since the confidence intervals established in (d) do not include the zero value.

(f) This hypothesis is equivalent to the hypothesis that $R^2 = 0$. It can be tested using the R^2 variant of the F test:

$$F = \frac{0.9988/2}{(1-0.9988)/12} = 4{,}994$$

This F value is obviously highly significant, leading to the rejection of the null of the null hypothesis. Set up the ANOVA table as indicated in the text.

8.9. (*a*) 15 (*b*) 77 (*c*) 2 and 12, respectively

(*d*) $R^2 = 0.9988$; $\bar{R}^2 = 0.9986$

(*e*) $F = \dfrac{65,965/2}{77/12} = 5,140.13$. This F value is highly significant, leading to the rejection of the null hypothesis

(*f*) No. We need the results of the two-variable regression models.

8.10. Follow Table 8-3 in the text.

8.11. (*a*) *Ceteris paribus*, if the BTU rating of an air conditioner goes up by a unit, the average price of the air conditioner goes up by about 2.3 cents. Other partial slope coefficients should be interpreted similarly. The intercept value has no viable economic meaning in the present case.

(*b*) Yes. *A priori*, each X variable is expected to have a positive impact on the price.

(*c*) For 15 d.f. the 5% one-tailed critical t value is 1.753. The observed t value of $0.023 / 0.005 = 4.6$ exceeds this critical t value. Hence, we reject the null hypothesis.

(*d*) $H_0: R^2 = 0$ and $H_1: R^2 > 0$. Using the F test, we obtain

$$F = \dfrac{0.84/3}{0.16/15} = 26.25$$

This F value is significant beyond the 0.01 level of significance. So, reject the null hypothesis.

8.12. (*a*) The MPC is 0.93.

(*b*) $t = \dfrac{0.93 - 1}{0.003734} = -18.7465$

For 73 d.f. this t value is highly significant. Hence reject the null hypothesis that the true MPC is unity (*Note*: The se is obtained as $0.93 / 249.06 = 0.003734$).

(*c*) Since expenditure on items such as automobiles, washers and dryers, etc., is often financed, the cost of borrowing becomes an important determinant of consumption expenditure. Therefore, the interest rate, representing the cost of borrowing, is expected to have a negative impact on consumption expenditure.

(*d*) Yes. The *t* value is -3.09, which is significant at about the 0.01 level of significance (two-tailed test).

(*e*) $F = \dfrac{0.9996/2}{(1-0.9996)/73} = 91,213.5$

This *F* value is obviously very high, leading to the rejection of the null hypothesis that $R^2 = 0$. (*Note*: The *F* value reported by the authors is different because of rounding.)

(*f*) se(b_1) = 3.2913;   se(b_2) = 0.003734;   se(b_3) = 0.6764.

8.13. Use the *F* test: $F = \dfrac{0.96/2}{(1-0.96)/16} = 192$

For 2 and 16 d.f., this *F* value is highly significant. Hence, reject the null hypothesis that X_2 and X_3 have no influence on *Y*. The *F* test assumes that the error term is distributed normally.

8.14. (*a*) CM is expected to be negatively related to FLR and PGNP but positively related to TFR.

(*b*) The *EViews* regression results are:

Dependent Variable: CM Sample: 1 64				
Variable	Coefficient	Std. Error	t-Statistic	Prob.
C	263.8635	12.22499	21.58395	0.0000
FLR	-2.390496	0.213263	-11.20917	0.0000
R-squared	0.669590			

(*c*) The regression output is:

(Regression output is shown in the following page)

Dependent Variable: CM				
Sample: 1 64				
Variable	Coefficient	Std. Error	t-Statistic	Prob.
C	263.6416	11.59318	22.74109	0.0000
FLR	-2.231586	0.209947	-10.62927	0.0000
PGNP	-0.005647	0.002003	-2.818703	0.0065
R-squared	0.707665			

(**d**) Adding the variable TFR, we obtain:

Dependent Variable: CM				
Sample: 1 64				
Variable	Coefficient	Std. Error	t-Statistic	Prob.
C	168.3067	32.89165	5.117003	0.0000
FLR	-1.768029	0.248017	-7.128663	0.0000
PGNP	-0.005511	0.001878	-2.934275	0.0047
TFR	12.86864	4.190533	3.070883	0.0032
R-squared	0.747372			

The ANOVA table is straightforward. Set it up using the R^2 value.

(**e**) The model in (*d*) seems to be better in that all the variables have the expected the expected signs, each variable is individually statistically significant since the *p* values are very low, and the overall R^2 value is fairly high for cross-sectional data.

(**f**) In each case we will be committing a specification error, namely, the error of omitting a relevant variable(s). As a result, the coefficients of the incorrectly estimated model are likely to be inconsistent, a topic explored in Chapter 11.

(**g**) To answer this question, we use Equation (8.56). In the present case the unrestricted coefficient of determination, R_{ur}^2 (i.e., model (*d*)) is 0.7474 (approx.) and the restricted coefficient of determination R_r^2 (i.e., model (*b*) is 0.6696 (approx.). The number of restrictions here is 2 because model (*b*) excludes 2 variables (PGNP and TFR). Using Equation (8.56), we get:

$$F = \frac{(0.7474 - 0.6696)/2}{(1 - 0.7474)/(64 - 4)} = \frac{0.03890}{0.00421} = 9.2399$$

For 2 numerator and 60 denominator d.f., the computed F value is highly significant (the 1 percent critical value is 4.98), suggesting that both PGNP and TFR belong in the model.

8.15. The adjusted R^2 values are shown in the last column of the following table:

Value of R^2	n	k	$\bar{R}^2$
0.83	50	6	0.8107
0.55	18	9	0.1500
0.33	16	12	-1.5125
0.12	1,200	32	0.0966

These calculations show that the $\bar{R}^2$ value depends on the sample size as well as on the number of explanatory variables in the model. If the sample size is rather small and if the number of explanatory variables is relatively large, the $\bar{R}^2$ can be substantially smaller than the (unadjusted) R^2, as the second example shows so clearly, or even negative, as in the third example.

8.16. Using formula (8.50), we obtain:

$$F = \frac{0.689/4}{(1-0.689)/15} = 8.3079$$

For 4 and 15 d.f., this F value is significant beyond the 0.01 level. Therefore, we can reject the hypothesis that $R^2 = 0$.

8.17. This is straightforward, but use the R^2 version of the ANOVA table.

8.18. (*a*) As a first pass, consider the following results obtained from *EViews*. The dependent variable is average starting pay (ASP).

Note: In this regression output, we present the adjusted R^2 for the first time.

(Regression output is shown in the following page)

Dependent Variable: ASP Sample: 1 47				
Variable	Coefficient	Std. Error	t-Statistic	Prob.
C	-47113.12	27181.07	-1.733306	0.0906
GMAT	0.563588	57.35432	0.009826	0.9922
GPA	15949.88	9945.821	1.603677	0.1165
PCTEMPLOYED	149.5466	88.18249	1.695876	0.0975
TUITION	0.578014	0.202868	2.849208	0.0068
RATING	13685.70	2720.399	5.030769	0.0000
R-squared	0.844132			
Adjusted R-squared	0.825124			

As these results suggest, GPA, tuition and recruiter perception have statistically significant positive impact on average starting salaries at the 10% or lower level of significance. The percentage of employed graduates also has a positive effect, indicating that higher demand for the graduates of a particular school translates into a higher salary. The R^2 value is reasonably high.

Note: This model does not include *all* the variables from Table 6.11.

(b) Since GPA and GMAT are likely to be collinear, if we introduce them both in the model, as in (*a*), we would not expect both the variables to be individually statistically significant. This is borne out by the results given in (*a*).

(c) If the tuition variable is a proxy for the quality of education, higher tuition may well have a positive impact on ASP, *ceteris paribus*. The results in (*a*) may support such a hypothesis.

(d) Regressing GMAT on GPA, we obtain the following *EViews* output:

Dependent Variable: GMAT Sample: 1 47				
Variable	Coefficient	Std. Error	t-Statistic	Prob.
C	198.3088	95.29500	2.080999	0.0432
GPA	140.5600	28.26825	4.972362	0.0000
R-squared	0.354602			
Adjusted R-squared	0.340260			

From these results it seems that GMAT and GPA are collinear.

(e) The *Excel* Analysis of Variance output is as follows (*EViews* does not automatically provide an ANOVA table in regressions):

Source of variation	SS	df	MSS	F	p-value
Regression	4,699,381,239.155	5	939,876,247.831	44.41	0.0000
Residual	867,733,763.313	41	21,164,238.130		
Total	5,567,115,002.468	46			

Note: In the source of variation, Regression is ESS, Residual is RSS, and Total is TSS.

Since the *p* value of the estimated *F* value is so virtually zero, we can conclude that collectively all the slope coefficients are not equal to zero, multicollinearity among some variables notwithstanding.

(f) Following the format of Table 8.3, we obtain:

Source of variation	SS	df	MSS	F	p-value
Regression	$0.8441(\sum y_i^2)$	5	$\dfrac{0.8441(\sum y_i^2)}{5}$	44.41	0.0000
Residual	$(1-0.8441)(\sum y_i^2)$	41	$\dfrac{(1-0.8441)(\sum y_i^2)}{41}$		
Total	$\sum y_i^2$	46			

Note: $\sum y_i^2 = 5,567,115,002.468$.

The conclusion is the same as before.

8.19. (a) It seems that way, because a straight line reasonably fits the residuals.

(b) No, it is not significant: The *p* value of obtaining the Anderson-Darling A^2 value of 0.481 or greater is about 20 percent. This supports the conclusion in (a) that the error term is normally distributed. See the discussion on normal probability plots in Chapter 7.

(c) The mean value is zero and the variance is 0.3412 (Divide the sum of the squared residuals by $n - 3 = 20$, since there are $n = 23$ observations in Table

1-1, on which the regression is based). Any minor differences between your regression output and the regression shown in the book are due to rounding.

8.20. Here are the raw data for calculations:

Dependent variable	Explanatory variable(s)	RSS
Auction price	None	4,803,756.7
Auction price	Age	2,245,713.7
Auction price	Number of bidders	4,059,311.8
Auction price	Age, number of bidders	525,462.2

In all the cases the total sum of squares is 4,803,756.7.

Note: The RSS can easily be obtained from the *EViews* regression outputs for the above regressions.

We compare the first model that has no explanatory variables since price is regressed only on the intercept ($RSS_r = 4,803,756.7$) with the model with all the explanatory variables ($RSS_{ur} = 525,462.2$). Applying the F formula given in this question, we obtain:

$$F = \frac{(4,803,756.7 - 525,462.2)/2}{(525,462.2)/(32-3)} = \frac{2,139,147.25}{18,119.38} \approx 118.058$$

This F value is about the same as in Equation (8.57), save the rounding errors.

CHAPTER 9

FUNCTIONAL FORMS OF REGRESSION MODELS

QUESTIONS

9.1. (*a*) In a log-log model the dependent and all explanatory variables are in the logarithmic form.

(*b*) In the log-lin model the dependent variable is in the logarithmic form but the explanatory variables are in the linear form.

(*c*) In the lin-log model the dependent variable is in the linear form, whereas the explanatory variables are in the logarithmic form.

(*d*) It is the percentage change in the value of one variable for a (small) percentage change in the value of another variable. For the log-log model, the slope coefficient of an explanatory variable gives a direct estimate of the elasticity coefficient of the dependent variable with respect to the given explanatory variable.

(*e*) For the lin-lin model, elasticity = $\text{slope}\left(\dfrac{X}{Y}\right)$. Therefore the elasticity will depend on the values of X and Y. But if we choose $\bar{X}$ and $\bar{Y}$, the mean values of X and Y, at which to measure the elasticity, the elasticity at mean values will be: $\text{slope}\left(\dfrac{\bar{X}}{\bar{Y}}\right)$.

9.2. The slope coefficient gives the rate of change in (mean) Y with respect to X, whereas the elasticity coefficient is the percentage change in (mean) Y for a (small) percentage change in X. The relationship between two is: Elasticity = $\text{slope}\left(\dfrac{X}{Y}\right)$. For the log-linear, or log-log, model only, the elasticity and slope coefficients are identical.

9.3. Model 1: $\ln Y_i = B_1 + B_2 \ln X_i$: If the scattergram of $\ln Y$ on $\ln X$ shows a linear relationship, then this model is appropriate. In practice, such models are used to estimate the elasticities, for the slope coefficient gives a direct estimate of the elasticity coefficient.

Model 2: $\ln Y_i = B_1 + B_2 X_i$: Such a model is generally used if the objective of the study is to measure the rate of growth of Y with respect to X. Often, the X variable represents time in such models.

Model 3: $Y_i = B_1 + B_2 \ln X_i$: If the objective is to find out the absolute change in Y for a relative or percentage change in X, this model is often chosen.

Model 4: $Y_i = B_1 + B_2(1/X_i)$: If the relationship between Y and X is curvilinear, as in the case of the Phillips curve, this model generally gives a good fit.

9.4. (*a*) Elasticity.

(*b*) The absolute change in the mean value of the dependent variable for a proportional change in the explanatory variable.

(*c*) The growth rate.

(*d*) $\dfrac{dY}{dX}\left(\dfrac{X}{Y}\right)$

(*e*) The percentage change in the quantity demanded for a (small) percentage change in the price.

(*f*) Greater than 1; less than 1.

9.5. (*a*) *True*. $\dfrac{d \ln Y}{d \ln X} = \dfrac{dY}{dX}\left(\dfrac{X}{Y}\right)$, which, by definition, is elasticity.

(*b*) *True*. For the two-variable linear model, the slope equals B_2 and the elasticity = slope $\left(\dfrac{X}{Y}\right) = B_2\left(\dfrac{X}{Y}\right)$, which varies from point to point. For the log-linear model, slope $= B_2\left(\dfrac{Y}{X}\right)$, which varies from point to point while the elasticity equals B_2. This can be generalized to a multiple regression model.

(c) *True.* To compare two or more R^2s, the dependent variable must be the same.

(d) *True.* The same reasoning as in (c).

(e) *False.* The two r^2 values are not directly comparable.

9.6. The elasticity coefficients for the various models are:

(a) $B_2(X_i/Y_i)$ (b) $-B_2(1/X_iY_i)$ (c) B_2

(d) $-B_2(1/X_i)$ (e) $B_2(1/Y_i)$ (f) $B_2(1/X_i)$

Model (a) assumes that the income elasticity is dependent on the levels of both income and consumption expenditure. If $B_2 > 0$, Models (b) and (d) give negative income elasticities. Hence, these models may be suitable for "inferior" goods. Model (c) gives constant elasticity at all levels of income, which may not be realistic for all consumption goods. Model (e) suggests that the income elasticity is independent of income, X, but is dependent on the level of consumption expenditure, Y. Finally, Model (f) suggests that the income elasticity is independent of consumption expenditure, Y, but is dependent on the level of income, X.

9.7 (a) Instantaneous growth: 3.02%;   5.30%;   4.56%;   1.14%.

(b) Compound growth: 3.07%;   5.44%;   4.67%;   1.15%.

(c) The difference is more apparent than real, for in one case we have annual data and in the other we have quarterly data. A quarterly growth rate of 1.14% is *about* equal to an annual growth rate of 4.56%.

PROBLEMS

9.8. (a) $MC = B_2 + 2B_3X_i + 3B_4X_i^2$

(b) $AVC = B_2 + B_3X_i + B_4X_i^2$

(c) $AC = B_1\left(\dfrac{1}{X_i}\right) + B_2 + B_3X_i + B_4X_i^2$

By way of an example based on actual numbers, the MC, AVC, and AC from Equation (9.33) are as follows:

$$MC = 63.4776 - 25.9230\, X_i + 2.8188\, X_i^2$$

$$AVC = 63.4776 - 12.9615\, X_i + 0.9396\, X_i^2$$

$$AC = 141.7667 \left(\frac{1}{X_i}\right) + 63.4776 - 12.9615\, X_i + 0.9396\, X_i^2$$

(d) The plot will show that they do indeed resemble the textbook U-shaped cost curves.

9.9. (a) $\left(\dfrac{1}{Y_i}\right) = B_1 + B_2 X_i$ (b) $\left(\dfrac{X_i}{Y_i}\right) = B_1 + B_2 X_i^2$

9.10. (a) In Model A, the slope coefficient of -0.4795 suggests that if the price of coffee per pound goes up by a dollar, the average consumption of coffee per day goes down by about half a cup. In Model B, the slope coefficient of -0.2530 suggests that if the price of coffee per pound goes up by 1%, the average consumption of coffee per day goes down by about 0.25%.

(b) Elasticity = $-0.4795 \left(\dfrac{1.11}{2.43}\right) = -0.2190$

(c) -0.2530

(d) The demand for coffee is price inelastic, since the absolute value of the two elasticity coefficients is less than 1.

(e) Antilog (0.7774) = 2.1758. In Model B, if the price of coffee were $1, on average, people would drink approximately 2.2 cups of coffee per day. [*Note*: Keep in mind that ln(1) = 0].

(f) We cannot compare the two r^2 values directly, since the dependent variables in the two models are different.

9.11. (a) *Ceteris paribus*, if the labor input increases by 1%, output, on average, increases by about 0.34%. The computed elasticity is different from 1, for

$$t = \frac{0.3397 - 1}{0.1857} = -3.5557$$

For 17 d.f., this *t* value is statistically significant at the 1% level of significance (two-tail test).

(**b**) *Ceteris paribus*, if the capital input increases by 1%, on average, output increases by about 0.85 %. This elasticity coefficient is statistically different from zero, but not from 1, because under the respective hypothesis, the computed *t* values are about 9.06 and -1.65, respectively.

(**c**) The antilog of -1.6524 = 0.1916. Thus, if the values of $X_2 = X_3 = 1$, then $Y = 0.1916$ or $(0.1916)(1,000,000) = 191,600$ pesos.

Of course, this does not have much economic meaning [*Note*: ln(1) = 0].

(**d**) Using the R^2 variant of the *F* test, the computed *F* value is:

$$F = \frac{0.995/2}{(1-0.995)/17} = 1,691.50$$

This *F* value is obviously highly significant. So, we can reject the null hypothesis that $B_2 = B_3 = 0$. The critical *F* value is $F_{2,17} = 6.11$ for $\alpha = 1\%$.

Note: The slight difference between the calculated *F* value here and the one shown in the text is due to rounding.

9.12. (**a**) *A priori*, the coefficients of ln(*Y* / *P*) and $\ln \sigma_{BP}$ should be positive and the coefficient of $\ln \sigma_{EX}$ should be negative. The results meet the prior expectations.

(**b**) Each partial slope coefficient is a partial elasticity, since it is a log-linear model.

(**c**) As the 1,120 observations are quite a large number, we can use the normal distribution to test the null hypothesis. At the 5% level of significance, the critical (standardized normal) *Z* value is 1.96. Since, in absolute value, each estimated *t* coefficient exceeds 1.96, each estimated coefficient is statistically different from zero.

(**d**) Use the *F* test. The author gives the *F* value as 1,151, which is highly statistically significant. So, reject the null hypothesis.

9.13. (**a**) If (1 / *X*) goes up by a unit, the average value of *Y* goes up by 8.7243.

(**b**) Under the null hypothesis, $t = \dfrac{8.7243}{2.8478} = 3.0635$, which is statistically significant at the 5% level. Hence reject the null hypothesis.

(c) Under the null hypothesis, $F_{1,15} = t_{15}^2$, which is the case here, save the rounding errors.

(d) For this model: slope $= -B_2\left(\dfrac{1}{X_t^2}\right) = -8.7243\left(\dfrac{1}{2.25}\right) = -3.8775$.

(e) Elasticity $= -B_2\left(\dfrac{1}{X_t Y_t}\right) = -8.7243\left(\dfrac{1}{(1.5)(4.8)}\right) = -1.2117$

Note: The slope and elasticity are evaluated at the mean values of X and Y.

(f) The computed F value is 9.39, which is significant at the 1% level, since for 1 and 15 d.f. the critical F value is 8.68. Hence reject the null hypothesis that $r^2 = 0$.

9.14. (a) The results of the four regressions are as follows:

	Dependent Variable	Intercept	Independent Variable	Goodness of Fit
1	$\hat{Y}_t =$	38.9690	$+ 0.2609 X_t$	$r^2 = 0.9423$
	$t =$	(10.105)	(15.655)	
2	$\ln Y_t =$	1.4041	$+ 0.5890 \ln X_t$	$r^2 = 0.9642$
	$t =$	(8.954)	(20.090)	
3	$\ln Y_t =$	3.9316	$+ 0.0028 X_t$	$r^2 = 0.9284$
	$t =$	(84.678)	(13.950)	
4	$\hat{Y}_t =$	-192.9661	$+ 54.2126 \ln X_t$	$r^2 = 0.9543$
	$t =$	(-11.781)	(17.703)	

(b) In Model (1), the slope coefficient gives the absolute change in the mean value of Y per unit change in X. In Model (2), the slope gives the elasticity coefficient. In Model (3) the slope gives the (instantaneous) rate of growth in (mean) Y per unit change in X. In Model (4), the slope gives the absolute change in mean Y for a relative change in X.

(c) 0.2609;   0.5890(Y/X);   0.0028(Y);   54.2126($1/X$).

(d) 0.2609(X/Y);   0.5890;   0.0028(X);   54.2126($1/Y$).

For the first, third and the fourth model, the elasticities at the mean values are, respectively, 0.5959, 0.6165, and 0.5623.

(e) The choice among the models ultimately depends on the end use of the model. Keep in mind that in comparing the r^2 values of the various models, the dependent variable must be in the same form.

9.15. (a) $\dfrac{\hat{1}}{Y_i} = 0.0130 + 0.0000833\, X_i$

$t = (17.206) \quad (5.683) \quad\quad\quad r^2 = 0.8015$

The slope coefficient gives the rate of change in mean $(1/Y)$ per unit change in X.

(b) $\dfrac{dY}{dX} = -\dfrac{B_2}{(B_1 + B_2 X_i)^2}$

At the mean value of X, $\bar{X} = 38.9$, this derivative is -0.3146.

(c) Elasticity $= \dfrac{dY}{dX}\left(\dfrac{X}{Y}\right)$. At $\bar{X} = 38.9$ and $\bar{Y} = 63.9$, this elasticity coefficient is -0.1915.

(d) $\hat{Y}_i = 55.4871 + 112.1797\left(\dfrac{1}{X_i}\right)$

$t = (17.409) \quad (4.245) \quad\quad\quad r^2 = 0.6925$

(e) No, because the dependent variables in the two models are different.

(f) Unless we know what Y and X stand for, it is difficult to say which model is better.

9.16. For the linear model, $r^2 = 0.99879$, and for the log-lin model, $r^2 = 0.99965$. Following the procedure described in the problem, $r^2 = 0.99968$, which is comparable with the $r^2 = 0.99879$.

9.17. (a) *Log-linear model*: The slope and elasticity coefficients are the same.
Log-lin model: The slope coefficient gives the growth rate.
Lin-log model: The slope coefficient gives the absolute change in GNP for a percentage in the money supply.

Linear-in-variable model: The slope coefficient gives the (absolute) rate of change in mean GNP for a unit change in the money supply.

(b) The elasticity coefficients for the four models are:

Log-linear: 0.9882

Log-lin (Growth):   1.0007 (at $\bar{X} = 1,755.667$)

Lin-log: 0.9260 (at $\bar{Y} = 2,791.473$)

Linear (LIV):   0.9637 (at $\bar{X} = 1,755.667$ and $\bar{Y} = 2,791.473$).

(c) The r^2s of the log-linear and log-lin models are comparable, as are the r^2s of the lin-log and linear (LIV) models.

(d) Judged by the usual criteria of the t test, r^2 values, and the elasticities, all the models more or less give similar results.

(e) From the log-linear model, we observe that for a 1% increase in the money supply, on the average, GNP increases by about 1%, the coefficient 0.9882 being statistically equal to 1. Perhaps this model supports the monetarist view. Since the elasticity coefficients of the other models are similar, it seems all the models support the monetarists.

9.18. (a) $\hat{Y}_t = 28.3407 + 0.9817 X_{2t} - 0.2595 X_{3t}$

se = (1.4127)   (0.0193)   (0.0152)

t = (20.0617) (50.7754)   (-17.0864) $R^2 = 0.9940$

p value = (0.0000)* (0.0000)*   (0.0000)* $\bar{R}^2 = 0.9934$

* Denotes a very small value.

(b) Per unit change in the real GDP index, on average, the energy demand index goes up by about 0.98 points, *ceteris paribus*. Per unit change in the energy price, the energy demand index goes down about 0.26 points, again holding all else constant.

(c) From the p values given in the above regression, all the partial regression coefficients are individually highly statistically significant.

(d) The values required to set up the ANOVA table are: TSS = 6,746.9887; ESS = 6,706.2863, and RSS = 40.7024. The computed F value is 1,647.638 with a p value of almost zero. Therefore, we can reject the null hypothesis that there is no relationship between energy demand, real GDP, and energy prices (*Note*: These ANOVA numbers can easily be calculated with the regression options in *Excel*).

(*e*) Mean value of demand = 84.370; mean value of real GDP = 89.626, and the mean value of energy price = 123.135, all in index form. Therefore, at the mean values, the elasticity of demand with respect to real GDP is 1.0428 and with respect to energy price, it is -0.3787.

(*f*) This is straightforward.

(*g*) The normal probability plot will show that the residuals from the regression model lie approximately on a straight line, indicating that the error term in the regression model seems to be normally distributed. The Anderson-Darling normality test gives an A^2 value of 0.502, whose *p* value is about 0.188, thereby supporting the normality assumption.

(*h*) The normality plot will show that the residuals do not lie on a straight line, suggesting that the normality assumption for the error term may not be tenable for the log-linear model. The computed Anderson-Darling A^2 is 1.020 with a *p* value of about 0.009, which is quite low.

Note: Any minor coefficient differences between this log-linear regression and the log-linear regression (9.12) are due to rounding. Regarding the Anderson-Darling test, it is available in *MINITAB*. If you do not have access to *MINITAB*, you can use the normal probability plots in *EViews* and *Excel* for a visual inspection, as described above. *EViews* also has the Jarque-Bera normality test, but you should avoid using it here because it is a large sample asymptotic test and the present data set has only 23 observations. In fact, the Jarque-Bera test will show that the residuals of both the linear and the log-linear regressions satisfy the normality assumption, which is not the case based on the Anderson-Darling A^2 and the normal probability plots.

(*i*) Since the linear model seems to satisfy the normality assumption, this model may be preferable to the log-linear model.

9.19. (*a*) This will make the model linear in the parameters.

(b) The slope coefficients in the two models are, respectively:

$$\frac{dY}{dt} = -\frac{B}{(A+Bt)^2} \quad \text{and} \quad -\frac{1}{Y^2}\frac{dY}{dt} = B$$

(c) In models (1) and (2) the slope coefficients are negative and are statistically significant, since the t values are so high. In both models the reciprocal of the loan amount has been decreasing over time. From the slope coefficients already given, we can compute the rate of change of loans over time.

(d) Divide the estimated coefficients by their t values to obtain the standard errors.

(e) Suppose for Model 1 we postulate that the true B coefficient is -0.14. Then, using the t test, we obtain:

$$t = \frac{-0.20 - (-0.14)}{0.0082} = -7.3171$$

This t value is statistically significant at the 1% level. Hence, it seems there is a difference in the loan activity of New York and non-New York banks. [*Note*: s.e. = (-0.20)/(-24.52) = 0.0082].

9.20. (a) For the reciprocal model, as Table 9-11 shows, the slope coefficient (i.e., the rate of change of Y with respect to X is $-B_2(1/X^2)$. In the present instance $B_2 = 0.0549$. Therefore, the value of the slope will depend on the value taken by the X variable.

(b) For this model the elasticity coefficient is $-B_2(1/XY)$. Obviously, this elasticity will depend on the chosen values of X and Y. Now, $\bar{X} = 28.375$ and $\bar{Y} = 0.4323$. Evaluating the elasticity at these means, we find it to be equal to -0.0045.

9.21. We have the following variable definitions:

TOTAL PCE (X) = Total personal consumption expenditure;

EXP SERVICES (Y_1) = Expenditure on services;

EXP DURABLES (Y_2) = Expenditure on durable goods;

EXP NONDURABLES (Y_3) = Expenditure on nondurable goods.

Plotting the data, we obtain the following scatter graphs:

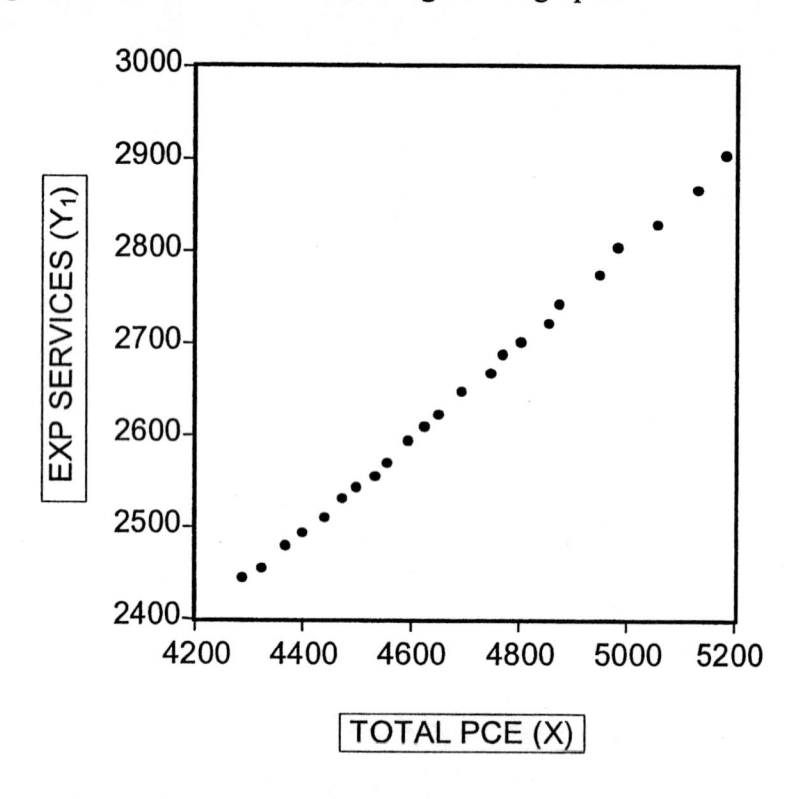

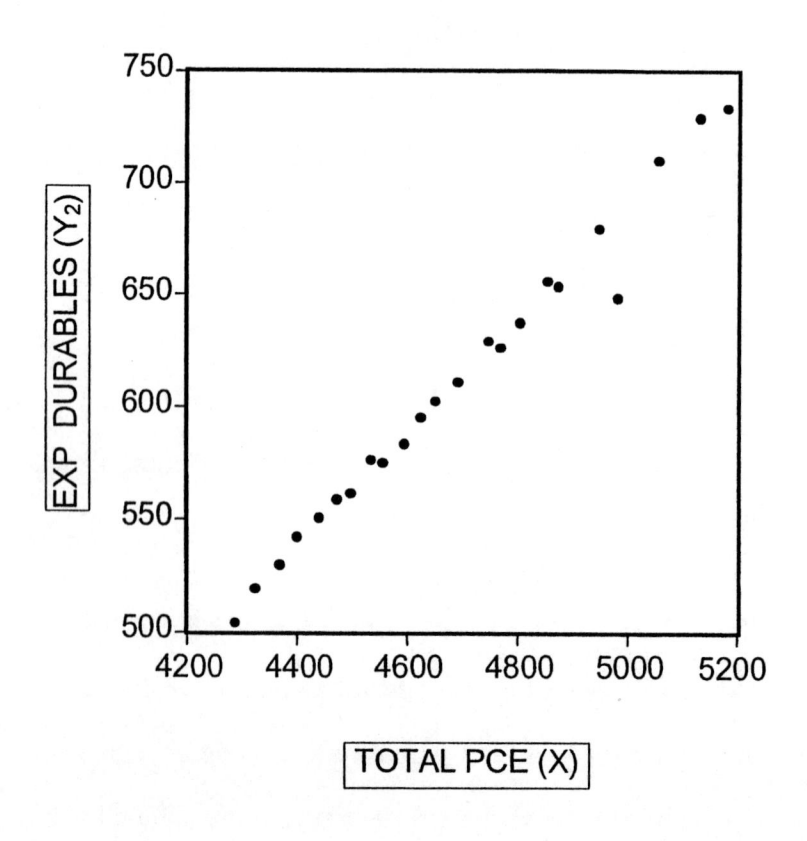

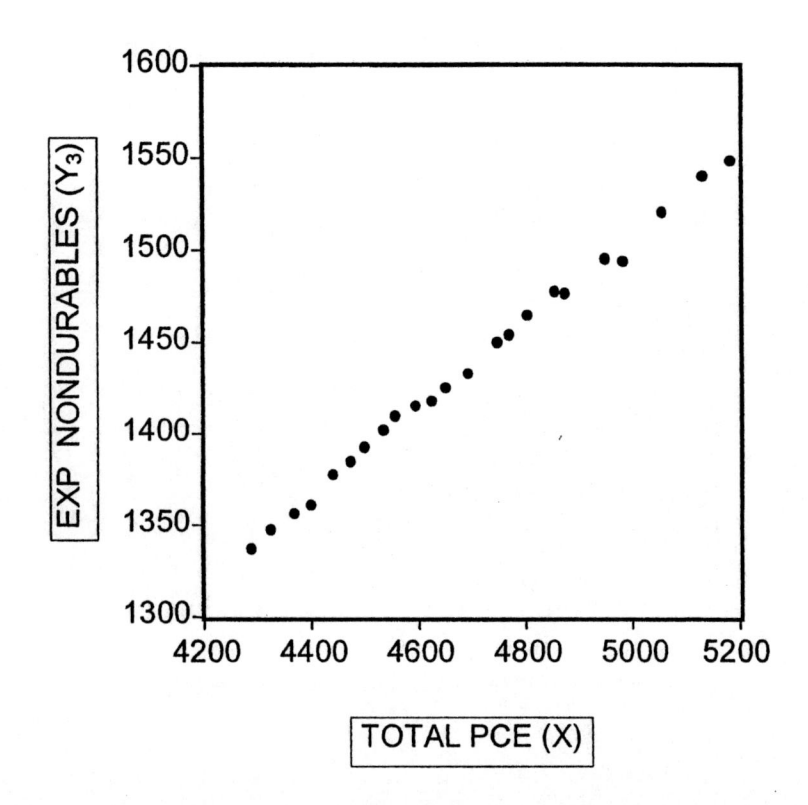

It seems that the relationship between the various expenditure categories and total personal consumption expenditure is approximately linear. Hence, as a first step one could apply the linear (in variables) model to the various categories. The regression results are as follows: (the independent variable is TOTAL PCE and figures in the parentheses are the estimated t values).

Dependent variable	EXP SERVICES (Y_1)	EXP DURABLES (Y_2)	EXP NONDURABLES (Y_3)
Intercept	222.5759 (11.9281)	-554.5943 (-16.8744)	335.7624 (24.7647)
Slope (TOTAL PCE)	0.5164 (129.8600)	0.2484 (35.4682)	0.2345 (81.1599)
R^2	0.9988	0.9836	0.9968

Judged by the usual criteria, the results seem satisfactory. In each case the slope coefficient represents the marginal propensity of expenditure (MPE) that is the additional expenditure for an additional dollar of TOTAL PCE.

This is highest for services, followed by durable and nondurable goods expenditures. By fitting a double-log model one can obtain the various elasticity coefficients.

9.22. The *EViews* results for the first model are as follows:

Dependent Variable: Y				
Sample: 1971 1980				
Variable	Coefficient	Std. Error	t-Statistic	Prob.
C	1.279719	7.688560	0.166445	0.8719
X	1.069084	0.238315	4.486004	0.0020
R-squared	0.715548			

The output for the regression-through-the-origin model is:

Dependent Variable: Y				
Sample: 1971 1980				
Variable	Coefficient	Std. Error	t-Statistic	Prob.
X	1.089912	0.191551	5.689922	0.0003
R-squared	0.714563			

- This R^2 may not be reliable.

Since the intercept in the first model is not statistically significant, we can choose the second model.

9.23. Using the raw r^2 formula, we obtain :

$$\text{raw } r^2 = \frac{(\sum X_i Y_i)^2}{\sum X_i^2 \sum Y_i^2} = \frac{(11,344.28)^2}{(10,408.44)(15,801.41)} = 0.7825$$

You can compare this with the intercept-present R^2 value of 0.7155.

9.24. Computations will show that the raw r^2 is 0.7318. The one in Equation (9.40) is 0.7353. There is not much difference between the two values. Any minor differences between regressions (9.39) and (9.40) in the text and the same regressions based on Table 6-12 are due to rounding.

CHAPTER 10

DUMMY VARIABLE REGRESSION MODELS

QUESTIONS

10.1. (a) and (b) These are variables that cannot be quantified on a cardinal scale. They usually denote the possession or nonpossession of an attribute, such as nationality, religion, sex, color, etc.

(c) Regression models in which explanatory variables are qualitative are known as ANOVA models.

(d) Regression models in which one or more explanatory variables are quantitative, although others may be qualitative, are known as ANCOVA models.

(e) In a regression model with an intercept, if a qualitative variable has m categories, one must introduce only $(m - 1)$ dummy variables. If we introduce m dummies in such a model, we fall into the dummy variable trap, that is, we cannot estimate the parameters of such models because of perfect (multi)collinearity.

(f) They tell whether the average value of the dependent variable varies from group to group.

(g) If the rate of change of the mean value of the dependent variable varies between categories, the differential slope dummies will point that out.

10.2. (a) Quantitative (b) qualitative (c) quantitative
(d) qualitative (e) quantitative (f) qualitative, if expressed in broad categories, but quantitative if expressed as years of schooling
(g) qualitative (h) qualitative (i) qualitative
(j) qualitative.

10.3. (a) If there is an intercept term in the model, 11 dummies.

(b) If there is an intercept term in the model, 5 dummies.

10.4. (*a*) Here we will fall into the *dummy variable trap*, because the four columns of the dummy variables will add up to the first column (representing the intercept).

(*b*) This equation can be written as:
$$GNP_t = B_1 + (B_2 + B_4)M_t + (B_3 - B_4)M_{t-1} + u_t$$
$$= B_1 + A_2 M_t + A_3 M_{t-1} + u_t$$

where $A_2 = (B_2 + B_4)$ and $A_3 = (B_3 - B_4)$.

Although we can estimate B_1, A_2, and A_3, we cannot estimate B_2, B_3, and B_4 uniquely. The problem here is that the third explanatory variable in the original model, $(M_t - M_{t-1})$, is a linear combination of M_t and M_{t-1}, thereby leading to perfect collinearity.

10.5. (*a*) *False*. Letting D take the values of (0, 2) will halve both the estimated B_2 and its standard error, leaving the t ratio unchanged.

(*b*) *False*. Since the dummy variables do not violate any of the assumptions of OLS, the estimators obtained by OLS are unbiased in small as well as large samples.

10.6. (*a*) Each regression coefficient is expected to be positive.

(*b*) B_2 tells us by how much the average salary of a Harvard MBA differs from the base category, which is non-Harvard and non-Wharton MBAs.

(*c*) It probably suggests that the Harvard MBA has a premium over the Wharton MBA.

10.7. (*a*) The model given in the previous question assumes that the average starting salaries of Harvard and Wharton MBAs are different from that of the other MBAs, but the rate of change of salary with respect to years of service is the same for all graduates. On the other hand, the model given in this question assumes that the average starting salary as well as the progression of salary (i.e., the rate of change) over years of service is different among Harvard, Wharton, and other MBAs.

(*b*) B_4 and B_5 are *differential slopes*.

(c) Yes, otherwise, we will be committing the "omission of relevant variable" bias.

(d) This can be tested by the F test.

PROBLEMS

10.8. (a) The coefficient -0.1647 is the own-price elasticity, 0.5115 is the income elasticity, and 0.1483 is the cross-price elasticity.

(b) It is inelastic because, in absolute value, the coefficient is less than one.

(c) Since the cross-price elasticity is positive, coffee and tea are substitute products.

(d) and (e) The trend coefficient of -0.0089 suggests that over the sample period coffee consumption had been declining at the quarterly rate of 0.89 percent. Among other things, the side effects of caffeine may have something to do with the decline.

(f) 0.5115.

(g) The estimated t value of the income elasticity coefficient is 1.23, which is not statistically significant. Therefore, it does not make much sense to test the hypothesis that it is not different from one.

(h) The dummies here perhaps represent seasonal effects, if any.

(i) Each dummy coefficient tells by how much the average value of $\ln Q$ is different from that of the base quarter, which is the fourth quarter. The actual values of the intercepts in the various quarters are, respectively, 1.1828, 1.1219, 1.2692, and 1.2789. Taking the antilogs of these values, we obtain: 3.2635, 3.0707, 3.5580, and 3.5927 as the average pounds of coffee consumed per capita in the first, second, third, and the fourth quarter, holding the values of the logs of all explanatory variables zero.

Note: On the general interpretation of the dummy variables in a semi-log model, see Robert Halvorsen and Raymond Palmquist, "The Interpretation of Dummy Variables in Semilogarithmic Equations," *The American Economic Review*, vol. 70 (June 1980), no.3, pp. 474-475.

(j) The dummy coefficients D_1 and D_2 are individually statistically significant.

(k) That seems to be the case in quarters one and two. Among other things, coffee prices and weather may have something to do with the observed seasonal pattern in these two quarters.

(l) The benchmark is the fourth quarter. If we choose another quarter for the base, the numerical values of the dummy coefficients will change.

(m) The implicit assumption that is made is that the partial slope coefficients do not change among quarters.

(n) We can incorporate *differential slope* dummies as follows:

$$\begin{aligned}
\ln Q = \ &B_1 + B_2 \ln P && + B_3 \ln I && + B_4 \ln P' && + B_5 T \\
&+ B_6 D_1 && + B_7 D_2 && + B_8 D_3 \\
&+ B_9 (D_1 \ln P) && + B_{10}(D_2 \ln P) && + B_{11}(D_3 \ln P) \\
&+ B_{12}(D_1 \ln I) && + B_{13}(D_2 \ln I) && + B_{14}(D_3 \ln I) \\
&+ B_{15}(D_1 \ln P') && + B_{16}(D_2 \ln P') && + B_{17}(D_3 \ln P') + u
\end{aligned}$$

Note: The subscript "t" has been omitted to avoid cluttering the equation. The first two rows of the equation are the same as in the text. The *differential slope* dummies are in the last three rows.

(o) One could estimate the model given in (*n*). If there are other substitutes for coffee, they can be brought in the model.

10.9. **(a)** It is a way of finding out if there are economies or diseconomies of scale. In general, if at a given point, the first derivative (i.e., the slope) is negative but the second derivative is positive, it means the slope is *negative* and *increasing*, that is, the negative slope tends to be less steep as the value of the variable increases.

(b) The same reasoning as in (*a*), except that miles has a positive sign and miles squared has a negative sign. In general, if at a given point, the first derivative is positive but the second derivative is negative, it means that the value of the function is increasing at a decreasing rate. In the present case, this is an indication of economies of scale, for the longer the distance in miles is, the lesser is the incremental fare.

(*c*) Population may be a proxy for traffic volume. The negative sign here indicates perhaps some type of economies of scale.

(*d*) Although negative, the coefficient is significant only for the "discount" category. This sign is rather puzzling.

(*e*) The negative sign makes economic sense in the sense that the higher the number of stopovers, the greater is the time spent traveling. Hence, the fare is lower to induce passengers to travel with several stopovers.

(*f*) It suggests that the average level of fare for Continental Airlines is lower than its competitors'.

(*g*) The critical Z value is 1.96 (5%, two-tailed) or 1.65 (5%, one tailed). If the computed Z value exceeds these critical values, the coefficient in question is statistically significant.

(*h*) Although this dummy coefficient is expected to be positive for all categories, it is not clear why it is significant only for the "discount" category.

(*i*) Yes, these observations can be pooled. In that case, introduce an additional dummy for the "coach" or "discount" fares.

(*j*) Overall, the results are a mixed bag. Although the R^2s are quite high for this sample size, and although several coefficients are statistically significant, some of the coefficients have dubious signs.

10.10. (*a*) Since the coefficient of the Dumsex dummy is statistically significant, Model 2 is preferable to Model 1.

(*b*) The error of omitting a relevant variable.

(*c*) *Ceteris paribus*, the average weight of males is greater than that of females.

(*d*) There is an additional variable, Dumht, in Model 3, which is statistically insignificant. As shown in Chapter 11, if an "unnecessary" variable is added to a model, the OLS estimators, while unbiased and consistent, are generally inefficient. This can be seen from Model 3. In Model 2 the Dumsex variable was statistically significant, but is insignificant in Model 3 because of the apparently superfluous Dumht variable. Also, keep in mind the possibility of multicollinearity.

(*e*) Choose Model 2. Not only is the Dumsex variable statistically significant in this model, but the coefficient of the height variable is about the same in both Models 2 and 3. On the other hand, neither dummy variable is statistically significant in Model 3.

(*f*) We observe from the correlation matrix that the coefficient of correlation between Dumsex and Dumht is very high, almost unity. As we show in the chapter on multicollinearity, in cases of very high collinearity, OLS estimators, although unbiased, have relatively large standard errors. Also, the signs and magnitudes of the coefficients can change with slight alterations in the data or in the specification of the model.

10.11. (*a*) $\widehat{Sales}_t = 4{,}767.750 + 912.250\, D_{2t} + 1{,}398.750\, D_{3t} + 2{,}909.750\, D_{4t}$

$t =\ $ (14.714)   (1.991)   (3.052)   (6.350)

$R^2 = 0.7790$

(*b*) The average sales in the first quarter was about \$4,768 million. In the second quarter it was higher by about \$912 million, in the third quarter by about \$1,399 million, and in the fourth quarter by about \$,2910 million, all these differences being statistically significant. The actual values of the intercepts in the various quarters can be obtained by adding the differential intercept dummies to the base quarter value. The individual intercept values are, respectively, (all in millions of dollars):

1st Quarter	2nd Quarter	3rd Quarter	4th Quarter
4,767.750	5,680.000	6,166.500	7,677.500

(*c*) To deseasonalize the data, subtract from each quarter's sales figure the dummy coefficient of that quarter. For instance, if you subtract from the sales figure for the fourth quarter of each year the number 2,909.750, the resulting figure for that quarter will indicate the seasonally adjusted sales for that quarter. Thus, the seasonally adjusted figures for the fourth quarter of 1983, 1984, 1985, and 1986 are as follows:

4th Quarter 1983	4th Quarter 1984	4th Quarter 1985	4th Quarter 1986
4,2002.250	4,294.250	5,077.250	5,697.250

10.12. (*a*) In this model, we have assigned a dummy coefficient for each quarter. But notice that, to avoid the dummy variable trap, we have omitted the intercept term from this model.

(*b*) Yes.

(*c*) $\hat{Sales}_t = 4{,}767.750\,D_{1t} + 5{,}680.000\,D_{2t} + 6{,}166.500\,D_{3t} + 7{,}677.500\,D_{4t}$

$t = \quad(14.714)\qquad\quad(17.529)\qquad\quad(19.030)\qquad\quad(23.693)$

This model gives directly the intercept values for all the four quarters, whereas, as shown in problem 10.11, the intercept values for the second, third, and fourth quarters were obtained by adding the differential intercept dummy values to the intercept value of the base quarter. Of course, both procedures give identical results, as they should.

Note: The R^2 value of this model is not presented for the reasons explained in the text (Ch. 9).

10.13. In this case the model will be:

$$AAS_i = B_1 + B_2 D_{2i} + B_3 D_{3i} + B_4 PPS_i + B_5(D_{2i} PPS_i) + B_6(D_{3i} PPS_i) + u_i$$

The *EViews* regression results are as follows:

```
Dependent Variable: PAY
Sample: 1 51
```

Variable	Coefficient	Std. Error	t-Statistic	Prob.
C	14625.33	1764.716	8.287640	0.0000
D2	-3950.555	3090.229	-1.278402	0.2077
D3	-5040.081	3075.927	-1.638557	0.1083
PPS	2.942800	0.420567	6.997216	0.0000
D2*PPS	0.582120	0.763982	0.761955	0.4501
D3*PPS	1.121671	0.860531	1.303464	0.1990
R-squared	0.733795	F-statistic		24.80849

Note: The dependent variable, "Pay", is the same as *AAS*: *AAS* is labeled "Pay" in Table 10-4, on which the example is based. The *F* statistic is also shown here as part of the *EViews* output for the first time.

Compared with Equation (10.17), these results suggest that there is no regional variation in the coefficient of *PPS*. Hence, the results of Equation (10.17) seem acceptable.

10.14. This can be accomplished by adding as variables the product of X_i and D_{2i} and the product of X_i and D_{3i}.

10.15. Using *EViews*, and suppressing the intercept to avoid the problem of perfect multicollinearity, we obtain the following results:

Dependent Variable: FRIG Sample: 1978:1 1985:4				
Variable	Coefficient	Std. Error	t-Statistic	Prob.
DUM1MINE	1222.125	59.99041	20.37200	0.0000
DUM2	1467.500	59.99041	24.46224	0.0000
DUM3	1569.750	59.99041	26.16668	0.0000
DUM4	1160.000	59.99041	19.33642	0.0000
R-squared	0.531797			

Here the various dummies represent the average sale of refrigerators in each quarter.

10.16. *(a)* By interaction we mean when both effects (sex and race) are present simultaneously.

(b) B_2 = differential effect of being a male

B_3 = differential effect of being white

B_4 = differential effect of being a white male

(c) $E(Y) = (B_1 + B_2 + B_3 + B_4) + B_5 X_i$

given that $D_{2i} = D_{3i} = 1$. Thus, a white male's mean annual salary is higher by B_4 as compared to the mean salary of a male alone or a white alone.

10.17. We define the new Sex dummy variable as equal to 1 for female and –1 for male and name it SEX1FN1M, to distinguish it from the original dummy variable SEX already in Table 10-2. In SEX1FN1M, "1FN1M" stands for 1 for female and negative 1 for male. The *EViews* output is as follows:

Dependent Variable: FOODEXP Sample: 1 12				
Variable	Coefficient	Std. Error	t-Statistic	Prob.
C	2925.250	164.7874	17.75166	0.0000
SEX1FN1M	-251.5833	164.7874	-1.526714	0.1578
R-squared	0.189026			

With this dummy setup, the constant term represents the "average" intercept of the regression line from which the female and male intercepts differ by 251.5833, in the opposite direction. Thus, the intercept for males is (2,925.250 + 251.5833) = 3,176.8333, and the one for females is calculated as (2,925.250 − 251.5833) = 2,673.6667, which are the values obtained for model (10.1) and shown in Equation (10.4), save any minor rounding errors.

10.18. In this problem, we define the new Sex dummy variable as equal to 2 for female and 1 for male and name it SEX2F1M, to distinguish it from the original dummy variable SEX already in Table 10-2. In SEX2F1M, "2F1M" stands for 2 for female and 1 for male. The regression results are:

Dependent Variable: FOODEXP Sample: 1 12				
Variable	Coefficient	Std. Error	t-Statistic	Prob.
C	3680.000	521.1036	7.061935	0.0000
SEX2F1M	-503.1667	329.5749	-1.526714	0.1578
R-squared	0.189026			

These results are precisely the same as in Equation (10.4), by noting that when $D_i = 2$ (female), the female intercept is 3,680.000 − 2(503.1667) = 2,673.6666 and the male intercept is 3,680.000 − 503.1667 = 3,176.8333.

10.19 (*a*) Based on the 19 observations, the *EViews* regression results are:

Dependent Variable: NDIV Sample: 1999:1 2003:3				
Variable	Coefficient	Std. Error	t-Statistic	Prob.
C	248.8055	31.89255	7.801368	0.0000
ATPROFITS	0.206553	0.049390	4.182100	0.0006
R-squared	0.507103			

As these results show, there is a statistically significant positive relationship between the two variables, an unsurprising finding.

(*b*), (*c*), and (*d*) We can introduce three dummies to distinguish four quarters and can also interact them with the profits variable. This exercise yielded no satisfactory results, since both the dummies and interaction terms were completely insignificant, suggesting that perhaps there is no seasonality involved. This makes sense, for most corporations do not change their dividends from quarter to quarter. It seems that there is no reason to consider explicitly seasonality in the present case.

10.20. The reference category (i.e., the category with 0 value for all dummies) is unmarried white male. Therefore, the intercept for this category is 0.501. All other variables remain the same. The intercept for white unmarried female is (0.501 + 0.140) = 0.641. Since the coefficient of DF is not statistically significant at the 5% level, it seems that there is no difference between the two categories in their intercept values. Other variables remain the same.

10.21. You will have to expand the model by including the product of each dummy variable with the other explanatory variables (6 in all). Thus you will have to add (6 × 3) = 18 additional variables to the model. But do not forget the principle of parsimony.

10.22. (*a*) Since the *p* value of the dummy coefficient is about 14%, it seems that product-differentiation does not lead to a higher rate of return.

(b) From (*a*) it is obvious that there is no statistical difference in the rate of return for firms that product-differentiate and the firms that do not.

(c) Perhaps. If we had the original data, we could verify this. Product differentiation is the result of advertising and marketing strategies. For details, see any industrial organization textbook.

(d) To the equation given, add the product of *D* with each of the explanatory variables. Thus, there will be three additional variables in the model.

10.23. **(a)** Since both the differential intercept and slope coefficients are statistically significant, the Phillips curve has changed between the two time periods. The regression models for the two periods derived from this regression are:

$$\underline{1958\text{--}1969}: \hat{Y}_t = (10.078 - 10.337) + (-17.549 + 38.137)\left(\frac{1}{X_t}\right)$$

$$= -0.259 + 20.588\left(\frac{1}{X_t}\right)$$

$$\underline{1970\text{--}1977}: \hat{Y}_t = 10.078 - 17.549\left(\frac{1}{X_t}\right)$$

What is striking about the latter period is that the slope coefficient is negative! This would imply a "positively" sloped Phillips Curve.

(b) The original Phillips curve may be dead but several attempts have been made to revive it. See any modern textbook on macroeconomics.

10.24. From Table 10.10 we observe that of the 40 observations, 6 observations have negative predicted values and 6 have predicted values in excess of 1. Hence, there are 12 incorrect predictions. Therefore,

$$\text{Count } R^2 = 28 / 40 = 0.7000.$$

The conventional R^2 value is 0.8047.

10.25. **(a)** A scatter plot will show that the three expenditure categories are linearly related to PCE.

(b) Since the data are seasonally adjusted, if you regress each expenditure category on PCE and include the dummy variables, the dummy coefficients are likely to be insignificant. This, in fact, turns out to be the case. But keep in mind that the method of seasonal adjustment used by the U.S. government is different from the dummy variable method.

Note: *EViews* provides seasonal adjustment options.

(c) By including the dummy variables unnecessarily, you will be committing the bias of including superfluous variables. As a result, the standard error of the PCE coefficient is likely to be overestimated, which will lower the t values.

CHAPTER 11

MODEL SELECTION: CRITERIA AND TESTS

QUESTIONS

11.1. Specification errors occur when the form of the relationship between the dependent variable and the explanatory variables is wrongly specified because of:
1. Exclusion of relevant variables from the model, or
2. Inclusion of redundant variables in the model, or
3. Incorrect functional form (e.g., a linear model is fitted whereas the true model is log-linear), or
4. Wrong specification of the error term.

Notice that one or more of these problems might coexist.

11.2. Specification errors arise because:
1. The researcher is not sure of the theory underlying his research;
2. The researcher is not aware of the previous work in the area;
3. The researcher does not have data on the variables relevant for the model.
4. Of errors of measurement in the data.

11.3. A good econometric model:
1. Should be parsimonious;
2. Should obtain unique estimates of the parameters of the model;
3. Should fit the data at hand reasonably well;
4. Should have the signs of the estimated coefficients in accordance with theoretical expectations, and
5. Should have good (out of sample) predictive power.

11.4. Exclusion of relevant variables; inclusion of irrelevant variables; wrong functional form; wrong specification of the error term. Yes, one or more specification errors can occur simultaneously.

11.5. If a variable(s) is wrongly excluded from a model, the coefficients of the variables included in the model can be biased as well as inconsistent, the error variance is incorrectly estimated, the standard errors of the variables included in the model can be biased, and the conventional hypothesis testing based on the t and F tests can be unreliable.

11.6. The "relevancy" of a variable depends on the theory underlying the model. Thus, in a demand function for money, income of the consumer, the interest rate, etc. are relevant variables but not, say, the amount of bananas produced in Mexico.

11.7. In the presence of the irrelevant variables, the OLS estimators are LUE (linear unbiased estimators) but not BLUE, that is, they are not efficient.

11.8 Since the inclusion of the irrelevant variables increases the standard errors of the coefficients, one may tend to accept the null hypothesis that a particular coefficient is zero, although in fact it may not be. Therefore, one should not include unnecessary variables in the model.

11.9. See answers to questions (11.7) and (11.8) above.

11.10. This is a common problem that one faces in any econometric analysis. Here theory should be the guide to model building. If the empirical results are not in accord with theory, one should be very wary of accepting those results, for in econometric model building our primary objective is to test a theory.

PROBLEMS

11.11. (a) $\ln \hat{Y}_t = -7.8439 + 0.7148 \ln X_{2t} + 1.1135 \ln X_{3t}$

$t = (-2.9270) \quad (4.6636) \quad\quad (3.7221) \quad\quad R^2 = 0.9837$

The output-labor and output-capital elasticities are, 0.7148 and 1.1135, respectively, and both are individually statistically significant at the 0.005 level (one-tail test).

(b) $\ln \hat{Y}_t = 2.0696 + 1.2576 \ln X_{2t}$

$t = (4.9541) \quad (18.9061) \quad\quad\quad\quad\quad\quad\quad r^2 = 0.9649$

Since we have excluded the capital input variable from this model, the estimated output-labor elasticity of 1.2576 is a biased estimate of the true elasticity; in (a), the true model, this estimate was 0.7148, which is much smaller than 1.2576.

As noted in the chapter, $E(a_2) = B_2 + B_3 b_{32}$, where b_{32} is the slope in the regression of $\ln X_3$ on $\ln X_2$, which in the present example is 0.48747. Using the estimated values in (a), we therefore see that:

$$E(a_2) = B_2 + B_3 b_{32} = 0.7148 + 1.1135\,(0.48747) = 1.2576.$$

Therefore, a_2 is biased upward.

(c) $\ln \hat{Y}_t = -19.2380 + 2.4409 \ln X_{3t}$

$t = (-10.8443)\quad (16.4554) \hspace{4cm} r^2 = 0.9542$

By excluding the relevant variable, labor, we are again committing a specification error. By the procedure outlined in (b), it is easy to show that:

$$E(a_3) = B_3 + B_2 b_{23} = 1.1135 + 0.7148(1.85712) = 2.4409,$$

where $b_{23} = 1.85712$.

This shows that the estimated elasticity is biased upward by 1.3274.

11.12. (a) Although most intermediate macroeconomics textbooks discuss the (Keynesian) consumption function as a function of income, there are economists who believe that wealth also is an important determinant of consumption expenditure. Therefore, the choice between Models I and II cannot be decided on purely theoretical grounds.

(b) Let Consumption $= C_1 + C_2$ Income $+ C_3$ Wealth $+ w$.

If in a concrete application both C_2 and C_3 turn out to be *individually* statistically significant, then neither Model I or Model II is the correct model. If, however, C_2 is significant and C_3 is not, probably Model I seems appropriate. On the other hand, if C_2 is insignificant but C_3 is significant, Model II may be appropriate. But beware of the problem of multicollinearity which is discussed in Chapter 12.

11.13. Here we commit the error of omitting a relevant variable, the intercept in the present instance. The consequences of omitting a relevant error are discussed in the chapter. Equation (9.40) gives the results of including the intercept in the model. In this particular instance the intercept term turns out to be statistically insignificant. Hence the results given in Equation (9.39) may be appropriate. In general, however, unless there is a strong reason to suppress the intercept, it is best to keep it in the model.

11.14. (a) $\hat{Y} = 23.9869 - 4.3756 X_3$

$t = (4.5820) \ (-4.2805)$ $\qquad r^2 = 0.4134$

(b) $\hat{Y} = 3.5318 + 3.9433 X_2 - 2.4994 X_3$

$t = (0.4354) \ (3.0487) \ (-2.3098)$ $\qquad R^2 = 0.5724.$

(c) That Fama is correct in his statement can be seen from the following regression:

(i) $\hat{Y} = -12.2815 + 5.6424 X_2$

$t = (-2.6137) \ (4.9099)$ $\qquad r^2 = 0.4811;$

(ii) $\hat{X}_2 = 5.1873 - 0.4758 X_3$

$t = (7.5055) \ (-3.5256)$ $\qquad r^2 = 0.3234.$

(d) First, the regression for 1954-1976 (that is, including 1954 and 1955) is:

$\hat{Y} = -1.3462 + 5.3231 X_2 - 2.6777 X_3$

$t = (-0.1657) \ (4.1037) \ (-2.1202)$ $\qquad R^2 = 0.6911.$

Dropping 1954 and 1955 and running the regression for 1956-76, we get:

$\hat{Y} = -11.3627 + 6.0120 X_2 - 1.0744 X_3$

$t = (-1.4726) \ (5.1418) \ (-0.9033)$ $\qquad R^2 = 0.7288.$

As a result of omitting just two observations, the regression results have changed dramatically. Inflation now has no statistically discernible effect on real rate of return on common stocks.

(e) Introducing $D = 0$ for observations in 1956-1976 and $D = 1$ for observations in 1977-1981, we obtained the following regression:

$$\hat{Y} = -3.3591 + 4.2531 X_2 - 1.6024 X_3 + 1.5156 D$$

$$t = (-0.3873) \quad (3.3337) \quad (-1.1646) \quad (0.1757) \quad R^2 = 0.5546.$$

Since the dummy coefficient is not statistically significant, there does not seem to be any difference in the behavior of real stock returns between the two periods. Of course, we are assuming that only intercepts differ between the two periods, but not the slopes. But this assumption can be tested by introducing a multiplicative dummy variable.

11.15. (*a*) The regression results for the four modes are as follows:

A:	$\ln Y_t = 1.5536 + 0.9976 \ln X_{2t} - 0.3328 \ln X_{3t}$ $t = (17.370) \ (52.606) \quad (-13.795)$ $R^2 = 0.9942$
B:	$\ln Y_t = 1.5932 + 0.8353 \ln X_{2t} + 0.1758 \ln X_{2(t-1)} - 0.3526 \ln X_{3t}$ $t = (12.219) \ (3.045) \quad (0.652) \quad (-12.511)$ $R^2 = 0.9942$
C:	$\ln Y_t = 1.6295 + 1.0058 \ln X_{2t} - 0.2363 \ln X_{3t} - 0.1208 \ln X_{3(t-1)}$ $t = (17.008) \ (52.027) \quad (-3.951) \quad (-1.920)$ $R^2 = 0.9950$
D:	$\ln Y_t = 1.2490 + 0.6713 \ln X_{2t} - 0.2704 \ln X_{3t} + 0.3332 \ln Y_{(t-1)}$ $t = (11.599) \ (6.593) \quad (-9.469) \quad (3.404)$ $R^2 = 0.9964$

(*b*) Omission of relevant variable bias.

(*c*) The income and price elasticities are as follows:

Model	Income Elasticity	Price Elasticity
A	0.9976	-0.3328
B	(0.8353 + 0.1758) = 1.0111	-0.3526
C	1.0058	(-0.2363) + (-0.1208) = -0.3571
D	0.6713 / 0.6668 = 1.0067	(-0.2704) / 0.6668 = -0.4055

(d) In the CLRM it is assumed that the explanatory variables are nonstochastic, that is, their values are fixed in repeated sampling. But if the lagged value of the dependent variable is one of the explanatory variables, this assumption cannot be met. As a result, as shown in Chapter 16, the usual OLS procedure may not be valid.

11.16. The results of the Cobb-Douglas production function including the trend variable are as follows:

$$\hat{\ln Y_t} = 4.9443 - 0.1218 \ln X_{2t} + 0.4034 \ln X_{3t} + 0.1181 X_{4t}$$
$$t = (1.2285) \quad (-0.4753) \quad\quad (1.3947) \quad\quad (3.6023)$$
$$R^2 = 0.9925$$

The trend variable is statistically significant at the 5% level. By not including the trend variable in the original model, we have committed the specification error of excluding a relevant variable. The consequence in the present example are clearly visible. Neither the labor input not the capital input seem to have any impact on output when the trend variable (perhaps denoting technology) is included in the model.

In this example, what is happening is that there is a significant trend in Y, X_2, and X_3. Therefore, what this regression shows is the relationship between output and the two inputs after the (common) trend in them has been removed. In other words, this regression gives the short-run relationship between output and labor and capital inputs, which in the present instance is not statistically significant.

Caution: The practice of introducing the trend variable in a regression has now come under scrutiny. The regression results presented here assume that the trend is *deterministic* and not *stochastic*. On this, see Chapter 16 where this topic is discussed at some length.

11.17. (*a*) The *EViews* output of the log-linear model is as follows:

| Dependent Variable: LOG(Y) |||||
| Sample: 1960 1982 |||||
Variable	Coefficient	Std. Error	t-Statistic	Prob.
C	2.189792	0.155715	14.06283	0.0000
LOG(X2)	0.342555	0.083266	4.113970	0.0007
LOG(X3)	-0.504592	0.110894	-4.550212	0.0002
LOG(X4)	0.148545	0.099673	1.490334	0.1535
LOG(X5)	0.091105	0.100716	0.904568	0.3776
R-squared	0.982313			

Note 1: A crucial point to remember: In *EViews*, the logarithmic functions are functions to the base e (natural logarithms). *EViews* uses the "log" term for such logarithms, even though natural logarithms are denoted with "ln" in general practice. So, in *EViews*, "log" stands for natural logarithm. If you want to convert a natural logarithm into one with the base 10, you should use the relationship: $\log_{10} x = \log_e x / \log_e 10$.

Note 2: In this example, there is a sixth variable, X_6, which is not used here as it is a composite of X_4 and X_5.

(*b*) Using EViews, we obtain the following linear model:

| Dependent Variable: Y |||||
| Sample: 1960 1982 |||||
Variable	Coefficient	Std. Error	t-Statistic	Prob.
C	37.23236	3.717695	10.01490	0.0000
X2	0.005011	0.004893	1.024083	0.3194
X3	-0.611174	0.162849	-3.753010	0.0015
X4	0.198409	0.063721	3.113734	0.0060
X5	0.069503	0.050987	1.363144	0.1896
R-squared	0.942580			

(*c*) We cannot directly compare the two models for reasons stated in the text. To choose between the two models, we can use the MWD test discussed in the text. After constructing variables Z_1 and Z_2 in the manner described in the text, we obtain the following regressions:

Dependent Variable: Y				
Sample: 1960 1982				
Variable	Coefficient	Std. Error	t-Statistic	Prob.
C	34.44709	2.137981	16.11197	0.0000
X2	0.002799	0.002775	1.008372	0.3274
X3	-0.489682	0.093635	-5.229701	0.0001
X4	0.162059	0.036315	4.462567	0.0003
X5	0.090554	0.028884	3.135118	0.0060
Z1	-50.13320	7.941861	-6.312526	0.0000
R-squared	0.982829			

Since the coefficient of Z_1 is statistically significant, we reject the linear model.

Dependent Variable: LOG(Y)				
Sample: 1960 1982				
Variable	Coefficient	Std. Error	t-Statistic	Prob.
C	2.164940	0.168893	12.81841	0.0000
LOG(X2)	0.340388	0.085330	3.989087	0.0009
LOG(X3)	-0.475355	0.131241	-3.621994	0.0021
LOG(X4)	0.129179	0.110943	1.164372	0.2604
LOG(X5)	0.094041	0.103256	0.910762	0.3752
Z2	-2.36E+09	5.33E+09	-0.443187	0.6632
R-squared	0.982515			

Note: -2.36E+09 and 5.33E+09 represent scientific notation.

Since the coefficient of Z_2 is not statistically significant, we do not reject the hypothesis that the true model is log-linear.

11.18. (*a*) The *EViews* results are as follows:

Dependent Variable: Y				
Sample: 1968 1987				
Variable	Coefficient	Std. Error	t-Statistic	Prob.
C	-655.0402	138.0686	-4.744308	0.0002
X	0.522760	0.089616	5.833365	0.0000
TIME	-20.70755	4.910361	-4.217114	0.0007
TIME*TIME	0.223554	0.129155	1.730898	0.1027
R-squared	0.970396			

(b) Since the time-squared term is borderline statistically significant (using an one-tail test, it is significant at the 10% level), model (11.13) is misspecified.

(c) In the present case we have omitted a significant variable from the model. As noted in the text, the presence of such a specification error leads not only to biased but also inconsistent estimates of the regression model that omits relevant variable(s). This can be seen from the regression results presented above.

11.19. If we include all the variables in the model as a startup model, we get the following *EViews* results:

Dependent Variable: MAP
Sample: 1 13

Variable	Coefficient	Std. Error	t-Statistic	Prob.
C	132.8086	48.79243	2.721910	0.0297
SPP	-0.001082	0.002687	-0.402874	0.6991
STR	2.794246	2.415948	1.156584	0.2854
EDU	0.795938	0.472978	1.682824	0.1363
MINCOME	0.000175	0.000316	0.554112	0.5968
DUM	21.60799	13.81711	1.563857	0.1618
R-squared	0.947735			

Since none of the explanatory variables is statistically significant, we have to rethink the initial model. It seems that we have multicollinearity in the variables.

(b), (c) and (d) Using only STR, EDU, and DUM as explanatory variables, we obtain the following results:

Dependent Variable: MAP
Sample: 1 13

Variable	Coefficient	Std. Error	t-Statistic	Prob.
C	114.0212	25.80188	4.419103	0.0017
STR	3.764235	1.555686	2.419663	0.0386
EDU	0.844971	0.272621	3.099430	0.0127
DUM	24.14025	10.42762	2.315029	0.0459
R-squared	0.944921			

You can try other variations. In the preceding regression all the variables are individually statistically significant. But the positive value of the STR coefficient would suggest that, *ceteris paribus*, the higher the student-teacher ratio, the higher the MAP. This is counter-intuitive.

It would seem both social and economic factors are important in the MAP test outcome.

11.20. Econometrically speaking, the Supreme Court's decision is incorrect, for the consequences of excluding relevant variables can be serious. Of course, the defendants in this case simply argued that the plaintiff's model had not included all the relevant variables. If the defendants were serious, they should have presented their own regression results to buttress their argument that as a result of omitting the relevant variables the results submitted by the plaintiffs were seriously biased. In the absence of such evidence, the Supreme Court did the best it could.

CHAPTER 12

MULTICOLLINEARITY: WHAT HAPPENS IF EXPLANATORY VARIABLES ARE CORRELATED?

QUESTIONS

12.1. An exact linear relationship between two or more (explanatory) variables; more than one exact linear relationship between two or more explanatory variables.

12.2. In perfect collinearity there is an *exact linear* relationship between two or more variables, whereas in imperfect collinearity this relationship is not exact but an approximate one.

12.3. Since 1 foot = 12 inches, there is an exact linear relationship between the variables "height in inches" and "height in feet", if both variables are included in the same regression. In this case, we have only one independent explanatory variable and not two.

12.4. Disagree. The variables X^2 and X^3 are *nonlinear* functions of X. Hence, their inclusion in the regression model does not violate the assumption of the classical linear regression model (CLRM) of "no exact *linear* relationship among explanatory variables."

12.5. Consider, for instance, Eq. (8.21). Let $x_{3i} = 2x_{2i}$. Substituting this into Equation (8.21), we obtain:

$$b_2 = \frac{(\sum yx_2)(4\sum x_2^2) - (2\sum yx_2)(2\sum x_2^2)}{(\sum x_2^2)(4\sum x_2^2) - (2\sum x_2^2)^2} = \frac{0}{0}$$

which is an indeterminate expression. The same is true of Equations (8.22), (8.25), and (8.27).

12.6. OLS estimators are still BLUE.

12.7. (1) Large variances and covariances of OLS estimators

(2) Wider confidence intervals

(3) Insignificant *t* ratios

(4) A high R^2 but few significant t ratios

(5) Sensitivity of OLS estimators and their standard errors to changes in the data.

(6) Wrong signs for regression coefficients.

(7) Difficulty in assessing the individual contributions of the explanatory variables to the ESS or R^2.

12.8. The VIF measures the increase in the variances OLS estimators as the degree of collinearity, as measured by R^2, increases. If the (explanatory) variables are uncorrelated, the least value of VIF is 1, but if the variables are perfectly correlated, VIF is infinite.

12.9. (*a*) large; small

(*b*) undefined; undefined

(*c*) variances

12.10. (*a*) *False.* In cases of perfect multicollinearity, OLS estimators are not even defined.

(*b*) *True.*

(*c*) *Uncertain.* A high R^2 can be offset by a low σ^2 or a high variance of the relevant explanatory variable included in the model, or both.

(*d*) *True.* A simple correlation between two explanatory variables may be high, but when account is taken of other explanatory variables in the model, the partial correlation between those two variables may be low.

(*e*) *Uncertain.* It is true only if the collinearity observed in the given sample continues to hold in the post sample period. If that is not the case, then this statement is false.

12.11. This is because business cycles and or trends (reflecting growth rates) dominate most economic time series. Therefore, in a regression of the consumer price index (CPI) on the money supply and the unemployment rate, the latter two variables are likely to exhibit collinearity.

12.12. (*a*) Yes. In the course of a business cycle, variables such as income at times t and $(t-1)$ usually tend to move in the same direction. Thus, in the upswing phase of a business cycle, income this period is generally greater than the income in the previous time period.

(b) There are various methods of resolving the problem, such as the Koyck transformation, or the first difference transformation. Some of these methods are discussed in Chapter 16.

PROBLEMS

12.13. (a) No, because $X_3 = 2X_2 - 1$, which is perfect collinearity.

(b) $Y = B_1 + B_2 X_2 + B_3(2X_2 - 1) + u$

$= A_1 + A_2 X_2 + u$

where $A_1 = (B_1 - B_3)$ and $A_2 = (B_2 + 2B_3)$.

If we regress Y on X_2, we can obtain estimates of the combinations of the Bs as shown above, but not individual estimates of the Bs. Incidentally, the regression of Y on X_2 is:

$$\hat{Y} = -12.0 + 2.0\ X_2$$

Therefore, $(B_1 - B_3) = -12.0$ and $(B_2 + 2B_3) = 2.0$.

12.14. (a) X_2 is a product specific price index, whereas X_3 is the general price index. It is possible that the two indexes may not move together if there is a lead-lag relationship between the two.

(b) It is an indicator of employment conditions in the labor markets. *Ceteris paribus*, the higher the level of employment, the higher the demand for automobiles will be.

(c) Since we are dealing with a log-linear model, the partial slope coefficients are partial elasticities of the dependent variable with respect to the given variables.

(d) Running the logarithmic regression with $\ln Y_t$ as the dependent variable, and including all the variables, we obtain the following results for the aggregate demand function for passenger cars:

Variable name	Coefficient	t value
Constant	11.0582	0.5086 **
$\ln X_{2t}$	1.9409	2.1099 **
$\ln X_{3t}$	-4.6815	-2.5475 *
$\ln X_{4t}$	2.7164	1.8438 **
$\ln X_{5t}$	-0.0259	-0.2106 **
$\ln X_{6t}$	-0.5821	-0.2496 **
$R^2 = 0.8551$		

* Significant at the 5% level (two-tailed);
** Not significant at the 5% level (two-tailed).

12.15. From the results given in problem 12.14, multicollinearity may be present in the data. First, the R^2 value is reasonably high, but only one t value is statistically significant. Second, the general price index (X_3) has a negative sign, but the new car price index (X_2) has a positive sign. The latter may not make economic sense. Thirdly, neither the income variable (X_4) nor the employment variable (X_6) has any impact on the demand for autos, a rather surprising result. The interest rate (X_5) is also insignificant.

12.16. If you regress the natural log of each explanatory variable on the natural logs of the remaining explanatory variables, you will find that the R^2s of all these auxiliary regressions are very high, as the following table shows:

Dependent variable	Independent variables	R^2
$\ln X_{2t}$	$\ln X_{3t}$, $\ln X_{4t}$, $\ln X_{5t}$, $\ln X_{6t}$	0.9963
$\ln X_{3t}$	$\ln X_{2t}$, $\ln X_{4t}$, $\ln X_{5t}$, $\ln X_{6t}$	0.9995
$\ln X_{4t}$	$\ln X_{2t}$, $\ln X_{3t}$, $\ln X_{5t}$, $\ln X_{6t}$	0.9995
$\ln X_{5t}$	$\ln X_{2t}$, $\ln X_{3t}$, $\ln X_{4t}$, $\ln X_{6t}$	0.8734
$\ln X_{6t}$	$\ln X_{2t}$, $\ln X_{3t}$, $\ln X_{4t}$, $\ln X_{5t}$	0.9961

12.17. The simple correlation matrix of the natural logs of the X variables is:

	$\ln X_{2t}$	$\ln X_{3t}$	$\ln X_{4t}$	$\ln X_{5t}$	$\ln X_{6t}$
$\ln X_{2t}$	1.0000				
$\ln X_{3t}$	0.9960	1.0000			
$\ln X_{4t}$	0.9931	0.9964	1.0000		
$\ln X_{5t}$	0.5850	0.6138	0.5850	1.0000	
$\ln X_{6t}$	0.9737	0.9740	0.9868	0.5995	1.0000

Since the civilian employment (X_6) and disposable personal income (X_4) are likely to move together, one of them can be dropped from the model; notice that the correlation between the logs of these two variables is 0.9868. Similarly, since the two price indexes X_2 and X_3 are also likely to move together, one of them can be dropped; the simple correlation between the logs of these variables is 0.9960. But keep in mind the warning given in the text that simple correlations are not infallible indicators of multicollinearity. Also, keep in mind the "omission of relevant variables" bias if we drop one or more of these variables.

12.18. The following models may be acceptable on the basis of the usual economic (i.e., signs of the variables) and statistical criteria:

$$\hat{\ln Y_t} = -22.104 - 1.038 \ln X_{2t} - 0.295 \ln X_{5t} + 3.244 \ln X_{6t}$$
$$t = (-2.640) \quad (-3.143) \quad (-4.002) \quad (3.719)$$
$$R^2 = 0.6849$$

$$\hat{\ln Y_t} = -27.755 - 0.904 \ln X_{3t} - 0.251 \ln X_{5t} + 3.692 \ln X_{6t}$$
$$t = (-3.876) \quad (-4.491) \quad (-4.074) \quad (5.165)$$
$$R^2 = 0.7857$$

Compared with the original model, these two models have the correct signs for the various coefficients and all the individual coefficients are statistically significant. It is true that the R^2s of the these two models are not as high as that of the original model. Therefore, for forecasting purposes the original model might be better, provided the collinearity observed in the sample continues in the future. But that is a big proviso.

12.19. Prices of used cars, expenditure on advertising, a dummy variable to represent regional variation, import restrictions on foreign cars, and special incentives offered by the auto manufacturers (e.g., zero-interest financing or instant cash rebates) are some of the relevant variables that may further explain the demand for automobiles. But keep in mind that we need many more observations to include all these variables, assuming that the data on some of these variables are available.

12.20. (*a*) The slope coefficients in the first model are partial elasticities. In the second model, the coefficients of log K and log H are, as well, elasticities. The coefficient of the trend variable, t, suggests that, holding other things constant, (the index of) production has been increasing at the annual rate of about 2.7%.

(*b*) The t values of the regression coefficients are, respectively, -3.600, 10.195, and 6.518. For 18 d.f., the t values are significant at the 5% level, since the critical t value is 2.101.

(*c*) The t values of the trend variable and log K are 1.333 and 1.381, respectively, which are not statistically significant.

(*d*) It may be that the trend variable (perhaps representing technology) and log K are collinear.

(*e*) Even though a high pairwise correlation does not necessarily suggest collinearity, sometimes this may be the case.

(*f*) This hypothesis can be rejected, for the F value (using the R^2 variant) is 45.3844, which is significant beyond the 1% level, for the 1% critical F value for 3 and 17 d.f, $F_{3,17}$, is 5.18.

(*g*) The returns to scale are: $0.887 + 0.893 = 1.780$, that is, increasing returns to scale.

12.21. For instance, we have:

$$\text{var}(b_2) = \frac{\sum x_{3i}^2}{(\sum x_{2i}^2)(\sum x_{3i}^2) - (\sum x_{2i}x_{3i})^2}\sigma^2$$

Now:
$$r_{23}^2 = \frac{(\sum x_{2i}x_{3i})^2}{(\sum x_{2i}^2)(\sum x_{3i}^2)}$$

Substituting the latter into the former, we obtain, after simple algebraic manipulations, Equation (12.12). The same holds true of Equation (12.13).

12.22. (a) $\hat{Y} = 24.3370 + 0.8716 X_2 - 0.0350 X_3$

$t = (3.8753)\quad (2.7726)\quad (-1.1604)\qquad R^2 = 0.9682$

(b) Collinearity may be present in the data, because despite the high R^2 value, only the coefficient of the income variable is statistically significant. In addition, the wealth coefficient has the wrong sign.

(c) $\hat{Y} = 24.4545 + 0.5091 X_2$

$t = (3.8128)\quad (14.2432)\qquad r^2 = 0.9621$

$\hat{Y} = 26.4520 + 0.0480 X_3$

$t = (3.1318)\quad (10.5752)\qquad r^2 = 0.9332$

Now individually both slope coefficients are statistically significant and they each have the correct sign.

(d) $\hat{X}_3 = -3.3636 + 10.3727 X_2$

$t = (-0.0456)\quad (25.2530)\qquad r^2 = 0.9876$

This regression shows that the two variables are highly collinear.

(e) We can drop either X_2 or X_3 from the model. But keep in mind that in that case we will be committing a specification error. The problem here is that our sample is too small to isolate the individual impact of income and wealth on consumption expenditure.

12.23. Let $Y' = Y - 0.9$ earnings. Using the data given in Table 12-1, we obtain:

$\hat{Y}' = -220.2613 - 0.3527 X_2$

$t = (-202.1192)\quad (-2.0080)\qquad r^2 = 0.9483$

These results are vastly different from the ones in Equation (12.8), showing that unless the prior information is reliable, one can obtain dubious results.

Note: The r^2 value given has been corrected so that it can be directly compared with the r^2 value obtained from Equation (12.8).

12.24. Use the formula: $F = \dfrac{R^2/3}{(1-R^2)/19}$, which follows the usual F distribution with 3 and 19 d.f., respectively, in the numerator and denominator. The results of the F test will show that all the R^2s shown in Table 12-4 are highly statistically significant (at the 1% level, $F_{3,19} = 5.01$).

12.25. In Problem 11.19 we showed that when all the explanatory variables are included in the model, there is collinearity among these explanatory variables. There we also gave another version of the model. Variables such as education and median household earnings are likely to be correlated, as per human capital theory of labor economics. Likewise, spending per pupil is likely to be correlated with median household income. Wealthier school districts generally spend more on schooling. It is left for the reader to develop suitable models taking into account these factors.

12.26. Including the required variables in the model, and using *EViews*, we obtained the following regression results:

Dependent Variable: ASP
Sample: 1 47

Variable	Coefficient	Std. Error	t-Statistic	Prob.
C	40785.41	36399.32	1.120499	0.2690
GPA	14967.73	9089.393	1.646725	0.1073
GMAT	-92.26804	60.34581	-1.528988	0.1339
PCTACCEPT	-339.5064	99.64694	-3.407093	0.0015
TUITION	0.474208	0.186054	2.548771	0.0147
RATING	13782.47	2429.597	5.672738	0.0000
R-squared	0.870004			

In addition, we can generate the Analysis of Variance output from *Excel*, which is as follows:

Source of variation	SS	df	MS	F	p-value
Regression	4,843,413,719.634	5	968,682,743.927	54.88	0.0000
Residual	723,701,282.834	41	17,651,250.801		
Total	5,567,115,002.468	46			

Note: In the source of variation, Regression is ESS, Residual is RSS, and Total is TSS.

As these results suggest, the coefficients of GPA and GMAT are not statistically significant, perhaps due to collinearity. There seems to be collinearity among other variables. If we include only the percentage accepted, tuition, and recruiter rating as variables, we get the following results:

Dependent Variable: ASP
Sample: 1 47

Variable	Coefficient	Std. Error	t-Statistic	Prob.
C	32480.13	9433.619	3.443019	0.0013
PCTACCEPT	-296.5601	80.44179	-3.686643	0.0006
TUITION	0.281774	0.154584	1.822789	0.0753
RATING	14041.90	2228.417	6.301288	0.0000
R-squared	0.859236			

You are invited to use the data to develop other models.

CHAPTER 13

HETEROSCEDASTICITY: WHAT HAPPENS IF THE ERROR VARIANCE IS NONCONSTANT?

QUESTIONS

13.1. Heteroscedasticity means that the variance of the error term in a regression model does not remain constant between observations.

(*a*) The OLS estimators are still unbiased but they are no longer efficient.

(*b*) and (*c*) Since the estimated standard errors of OLS estimators may be biased, the resulting *t* ratios are likely to be biased too. As a result, the usual confidence intervals, hypothesis testing procedure, etc. are likely to be of questionable value.

13.2. (*a*) *False*. The OLS estimators are still unbiased; only they are no longer efficient.

(*b*) *True*. Since the estimated standard errors are likely to be biased, the *t* ratios will be biased too.

(*c*) *False*. Sometimes OLS overestimates the variances of OLS estimators and sometimes it underestimates them.

(*d*) *Uncertain*. It may or may not. Sometimes a systematic pattern in the residuals may reflect specification bias, such as omission of a relevant variable, or wrong functional form, etc.

(*e*) *True*. Since the true heteroscedastic variances are not directly observable, one cannot test for heteroscedasticity directly without making some assumptions.

13.3. (*a*) Yes, because of the diversity of firms included in the Fortune 500 list.

(*b*) Probably.

(*c*) Probably not. In time series data, it is often not easy to isolate the effects of autocorrelation and heteroscedasticity.

(*d*) Yes, because of vast differences in per capita income data of developed and developing countries.

(e) Yes. Although the U.S. and Canadian inflation rates are similar, the Latin American countries exhibit wide swings in the inflation rate.

13.4. By giving unequal weights, WLS discounts extreme observations. The estimators thus obtained are BLUE. Note that WLS is a specific application of GLS, the method of generalized least squares.

13.5. (a) This is a visual method, which is often a good starting point to find out if one or more assumptions of the classical linear regression model (CLRM) are fulfilled.

(b) and (c) These two tests formalize the graphical method by making suitable assumptions(s) about the explanatory variable(s) that might be the cause of heteroscedasticity.

PROBLEMS

13.6. Let $Y_i = B_1 + B_2 X_i + u_i$. Now divide this equation through by X_i^2 to obtain:

$$\frac{Y_i}{X_i^2} = B_1 \frac{1}{X_i^2} + B_2 \frac{1}{X_i} + v_i, \text{ where } v_i = \frac{u_i}{X_i^2}$$

The error term v_i is homoscedastic. Use the regression-through-the-origin procedure to estimate the parameters of the transformed model.

13.7. (a) Perhaps heteroscedasticity is present in the data.

(b) $\text{var}(u_i) = \sigma^2 (\text{GNP}_i^2)$.

(c) The coefficients of the original and transformed models are about the same, although the standard errors of the coefficients in the transformed model seem to be somewhat lower, perhaps suggesting that the authors have succeeded in reducing the severity of heteroscedasticity.

(d) No. In the transformed model, the intercept in fact represents the slope coefficient of GNP.

(e) The two R^2s cannot be compared directly because the dependent variables in the two models are different.

13.8. (a) He is assuming that $\text{var}(u_i) = \sigma^2 X_i$, that is, the error variance is proportional to the distance from the central business district.

(b) Although the values of the slope coefficient in the original and transformed models are about equal, the standard error in the transformed model is lower (i.e., the *t* ratio is higher). This might suggest that the author has probably succeeded in reducing heteroscedasticity.

(c) The original model is a log-lin model. The slope coefficient of about -0.24 suggests that as the distance traveled from the central business district increases by a mile, the average population density decreases by about 24%. The results make economic sense because the greater the distance one has to travel to get to work, the lesser will be the density of population of that place.

13.9. **(a)** Because of earlier data errors, the regression results shown in equation (13.30) in the text are not correct. Based on the data in Table 13-2, the results are as follows:

$$\widehat{\ln Y_i} = -7.2822 + 1.3144 \ \ln Sales_i$$

$$se = (1.8615) \quad (0.1692)$$

$$t = (-3.9120) \quad (7.7674) \qquad r^2 = 0.7904$$

(b) The plots do not suggest strong heteroscedasticity.

(c) *Park Test:* $\widehat{\ln e_i^2} = -17.5539 + 6.6255 \ln(\ln Sales_i)$

$$t = (-1.8161) \quad (1.6387) \qquad r^2 = 0.1437$$

Note: The original regression is double-logarithmic. Therefore, in the Park test we are using the natural log of the squared residuals and the natural log of ln*Sales*.

Since the slope coefficient in this regression is not statistically significant at the 5% level, the Park test does not suggest the presence of heteroscedasticity.

Glejser Test: $|e_i| = -1.0771 + 0.1513 \ \ln Sales_i$

$$t = (-1.0700) \quad (1.6534) \qquad r^2 = 0.1459$$

This particular form of the Glejser test suggests that there is no heteroscedasticity.

(d) In the present case, the question is academic.

(e) Perhaps the log-linear model.

(f) No, because the dependent variables in the two models are not the same.

13.10. (a) $\widehat{R\&D}_i = 77.5770 + 0.3614 \text{ Profits}_i$

$$t = (0.0789) \quad (3.9806) \qquad r^2 = 0.4976$$

$\widehat{\ln R\&D}_i = -1.2551 + 0.9910 \ln \text{Profits}_i$

$$t = (-0.9197) \ (6.2043) \qquad r^2 = 0.7064$$

(b) In the linear model there seems to be some evidence of heteroscedasticity. In the log-linear model such an evidence is not clear.

(c) *Linear Model*:

(1) *Park Test*: $\widehat{\ln e_i^2} = -7.8314 + 2.4958 \ln \text{Profits}_i$

$$t = (-2.1453) \ (5.8419) \qquad r^2 = 0.6808$$

Since the estimated t value is significant, the Park test suggests heteroscedasticity.

(2) *Glejser test*: $\widehat{|e_i|} = -25.4044 + 0.2172 \text{ Profits}_i$

$$t = (-0.0637) \quad (5.9043) \qquad r^2 = 0.6854$$

Again, there is indication of heteroscedasticity, since the estimated t value of profits is statistically significant. If you repeat the Park and Glejser tests for the log-linear model, you will find that the regression results are not significant.

(d) From the regression results for the linear model given in (a) it seems that in the regression of R&D on profits, the variance of the error term seems proportional to profits. In fact, he scatter diagram of profits and the regression residuals looks like Figure 13.8 in the text. Therefore, regress $(R\&D/\sqrt{\text{Profits}})$ on $(1/\sqrt{\text{Profits}})$ and $\sqrt{\text{Profits}}$. The results of this regression are:

$$\left(\frac{\widehat{R\&D}}{\sqrt{\text{Profits}}}\right)_i = -22.0242 \left(\frac{1}{\sqrt{\text{Profits}}}\right)_i + 0.3735 (\sqrt{\text{Profits}})_i$$

$$t = (-0.0969) \qquad (5.7057)$$

$$r^2 = 0.3592$$

Note: This regression has no intercept. Keep this in mind when interpreting the r^2 shown.

13.11. (*a*) Let Y = GDP growth rate (%), and $X = \dfrac{\text{Investment}}{\text{GDP}}$ (%).

You can regress Y on X. You can also regress ln Y on ln X, provided the Y values are positive. To make all the Y values positive, add a constant in such a way that the largest negative value becomes positive.

(*b*) Yes, there is evidence of heteroscedasticity. This should not be surprising because the countries in the sample have positive as well as negative real interest rates.

(*c*) If it is assumed that the error variance is proportional to the value of X, use the square root transformation. If it is assumed that the error variance is proportional to the square of X, divide the equation by X on both sides.

(*d*) Add two dummy variables to the model to distinguish the three categories of interest rate experiences. If the original model (without the dummies) was mis-specified, and if the residuals in the new model (i.e., with the dummies added) do not exhibit any systematic pattern, the "heteroscedasticity" observed in the original model can then be attributed to the mis-specification bias.

13.12. Let Y = median salary and X = age (Assume X = 72 for the last group).

(*a*) $\hat{Y} = 6{,}419.8182 + 127.8182\, X$

$t =$ (3.6408)   (3.5946) $r^2 = 0.5894$

(*b*) $\dfrac{Y}{\sqrt{X}} = 5{,}133.8548 \left(\dfrac{1}{\sqrt{X}}\right) + 155.1791\sqrt{X}$

$t =$ (3.6702)   (4.8764) $r^2 = 0.9608$

Note: This is a regression without an intercept. The r^2 shown is based on the raw r^2 formula. The original r^2 in *EViews* is negative, a common occurrence when the intercept is suppressed.

(*c*) $\dfrac{Y}{X} = 4{,}216.9105 \left(\dfrac{1}{X}\right) + 177.4836$

$t =$ (3.8596)   (6.2138) $r^2 = 0.6234$

(d) It seems that transformations (b) and (c) have reduced the standard errors in relation to the coefficients, probably reducing the heteroscedasticity problem. Plot the residuals from regressions (b) and (c) and see if they exhibit any systematic patterns. If they do, use the Park or Glejser test to further confirm if there is evidence of heteroscedasticity in the data.

13.13. The Spearman's rank correlation coefficient is 0.4407. Substituting this value in the given formula, the t value is 1.9636. For 16 d.f., the 5% one-tailed critical t value is 1.746. Therefore, the observed t value is significant at this level, suggesting perhaps that there is evidence of heteroscedasticity in the data.

13.14. (a) $\hat{Y}_i = 1{,}993.7258 + 0.2328 X_i$

$t = (2.1309) \quad (2.3340) \quad\quad\quad r^2 = 0.4376$

(b) $\dfrac{Y_i}{\sigma_i} = 2{,}417.3347\left(\dfrac{1}{\sigma_i}\right) + 0.1800\left(\dfrac{X_i}{\sigma_i}\right)$

$t = (2.1131) \quad (1.4273) \quad\quad\quad r^2 = 0.6482$

Note: This r^2 is the one generated by *EViews*. Since the regression does not have an intercept, you may wish to calculate the raw r^2 as an exercise.

In this example, the unweighted regression may be more appropriate based on the statistical significance of the coefficients.

13.15. $\operatorname{var}(v_i) = \operatorname{var}\left(\dfrac{u_i}{X_i}\right) = \dfrac{\operatorname{var}(u_i)}{X_i^2} = \dfrac{\sigma^2 X_i^2}{X_i^2} = \sigma^2$

13.16. (a) In regression (1) the slope coefficient suggests that if the number of employees increases by 1, the average salary goes up by 0.009 dollars. After multiplying through by N, the slope coefficient in model (2) is about the same as in model (1).

(b) The author is not only assuming heteroscedasticity, but specifically states that the error variance is proportional to the square of N.

(c) As noted in (a), the two slopes and the two intercepts are about the same.

(d) Because the two dependent variables are not the same, the two R^2s cannot be compared directly.

13.17. The derived average and marginal cost functions are as follows:

Average cost function [From Eq. (13.32)]:

$$\left(\frac{Y_i}{X_i}\right) = 476{,}000\left(\frac{1}{X_i}\right) + 31.348 - (1.083 \times 10^{-6})X_i$$

Marginal cost function [from Eq.(13.32)]:

$$\left(\frac{dY_i}{dX_i}\right) = 31.348 - 2(1.083 \times 10^{-6})X_i$$

Average cost function [from Eq.(13.33)]:

$$\left(\frac{Y_i}{X_i}\right) = 342{,}000\left(\frac{1}{X_i}\right) + 25.57 + (4.34 \times 10^{-6})X_i$$

Marginal cost function [from Eq. (13.33)]:

$$\left(\frac{dY_i}{dX_i}\right) = 25.57 + 2(4.34 \times 10^{-6})X_i$$

In Model (13.33) the quadratic term in X is not statistically significant, suggesting that the total cost function is linear. This means the average and marginal cost functions derived from (13.33) are in fact:

$$\text{Average cost} = \frac{342{,}000}{X} + 25.57$$

$$\text{Marginal cost} = 25.57$$

Note: If you need to refresh your memory on the concepts of various cost functions, consult any introductory microeconomics textbook.

13.18. (a) *A priori,* calorie intake should have a negative effect on infant mortality and population growth should have a positive effect.

(b) The *EViews* regression results are as follows:

(Regression output is shown on the following page)

Dependent Variable: IMOR				
Sample: 1 20				
Variable	Coefficient	Std. Error	t-Statistic	Prob.
C	172.6195	52.45598	3.290749	0.0050
PCGNP	-0.002502	0.001535	-1.629641	0.1240
PEDU	-1.279618	0.316722	-4.040198	0.0011
POPGROWTH	6.379603	7.045706	0.905460	0.3795
CSPC	-0.001363	0.018708	-0.072873	0.9429
R-squared	0.815002	F-statistic		16.52053
Adjusted R-squared	0.765670	Prob(F-statistic)		0.000023

Note: We are showing the *F* statistic and its *p* value here.

The population growth and calorie intake variables have the expected signs.

(c) Only one of the coefficients in the preceding regression is statistically significant, yet the *F* value is very significant. This seems to be a classic case of multicollinearity. Dropping the population growth (POPGROWTH) and per capita GNP (PCGNP) variables, the results were as follows:

Dependent Variable: IMOR				
Sample: 1 20				
Variable	Coefficient	Std. Error	t-Statistic	Prob.
C	250.0996	28.19164	8.871411	0.0000
PEDU	-1.210991	0.329756	-3.672385	0.0019
CSPC	-0.030999	0.013099	-2.366448	0.0301
R-squared	0.760462	F-statistic		26.98494
Adjusted R-squared	0.732281	Prob(F-statistic)		0.000005

Now both independent variables are statistically significant.

13.19. **(a)** The regression results show that the none of the coefficients in the auxiliary regression are statistically significant.

(b) Since not only the coefficients are insignificant but also the product of the R^2 and the sample size will not exceed the critical χ^2 value at 5 d.f., we can conclude there is no evidence of heteroscedasticity.

(c) Examine the residuals from the transformed model visually. You can also apply the White procedure to the residuals from the transformed regressions to make sure that they are not heteroscedastic.

13.20. (*a*) To explain the caloric intake, a model using the variables per capita GNP (PCGNP, or X_2), index of literacy (PEDU, or X_3), and population growth (POPGROWTH, or X_4) was developed. X_4 was insignificant and was dropped from the model, and the final *EViews* model was as follows:

Dependent Variable: CSPC
Sample: 1 20

Variable	Coefficient	Std. Error	t-Statistic	Prob.
C	1497.320	313.2984	4.779214	0.0002
PCGNP	0.060858	0.014767	4.121147	0.0007
PEDU	10.61977	3.556400	2.986102	0.0083
R-squared	0.716941			

(*b*) When plotted against the independent variables, the residuals from the preceding regression model showed visible heteroscedastic patterns.

(*c*) Using *EViews*, the following White's heteroscedasticity-corrected regression was obtained:

Dependent Variable: CSPC
Sample: 1 20
White Heteroskedasticity-Consistent Standard Errors & Covariance

Variable	Coefficient	Std. Error	t-Statistic	Prob.
C	1497.320	333.8182	4.485436	0.0003
PCGNP	0.060858	0.009457	6.435356	0.0000
PEDU	10.61977	3.855596	2.754379	0.0135
R-squared	0.716941			

As you can see comparing this regression with the one given in (*a*), the standard errors using the White procedure are different, in one case much lower and in the other a bit higher. That is, this procedure gives more efficient estimates of the parameters while allowing us to retain the original regression estimates.

13.21. Consider Model 1 in Table 11-2. Applying White's heteroscedasticity test (with no cross-product terms), we get the following results from *EViews*:

(Regression output is shown on the following page)

White Heteroskedasticity Test:				
F-statistic	3.214078	Probability		0.016850
Obs*R-squared	11.76858	Probability		0.019158

Test Equation:
Dependent Variable: RESID^2
Sample: 1 85

Variable	Coefficient	Std. Error	t-Statistic	Prob.
C	-42.97513	32.53147	-1.321033	0.1903
INCOME	0.002603	0.004075	0.638917	0.5247
INCOME^2	-1.72E-07	2.13E-07	-0.804801	0.4233
ACCESS	2.807384	1.124675	2.496174	0.0146
ACCESS^2	-0.023232	0.009280	-2.503543	0.0143
R-squared	0.138454			

Note: RESID^2 means residuals squared, and so on. The White χ^2 test statistic is also shown (Obs*R-squared), and it is significant (its p value is 0.0191). Incidentally, even if we introduce the cross-product terms, there is evidence of heteroscedasticity. When running the initial regression, do not forget to save your residuals in a new series so that you can apply the White test or other tests: The RESID series in each *EViews* work file is used as a depository of the residuals from each regression you run, and each new regression overwrites the residuals of the previous one.

These results suggest that we have a heteroscedasticity problem. One can use a variety of transformations to resolve it. You are urged to plot the squared residuals of the chosen model on each of the explanatory variables and / or on the estimated values of the dependent variable to see which variable might be used to transform the data to eliminate heteroscedasticity. We will give here the results of White's heteroscedasticity-corrected standard errors for Model 1 of Table 11.2, which are as follows:

Dependent Variable: LE
Sample: 1 85
White Heteroskedasticity-Consistent Standard Errors & Covariance

Variable	Coefficient	Std. Error	t-Statistic	Prob.
C	39.43802	1.823039	21.63313	0.0000
INCOME	0.000542	9.52E-05	5.695746	0.0000
ACCESS	0.283303	0.026132	10.84117	0.0000
R-squared	0.774146			

A comparison with the results given in Table 11-2 will show that apparently the original model overestimated the standard errors, for the estimated t values are lower in that table as compared with the t values shown in the preceding regression.

You can proceed similarly with the remaining two models in Table 11-2.

CHAPTER 14

AUTOCORRELATION: WHAT HAPPENS IF ERROR TERMS ARE CORRELATED?

QUESTIONS

14.1. (*a*) The correlation between the current value of the error with its own past value(s).

(*b*) The correlation between the current value of the error with its immediate past value.

(*c*) The correlation between observations over space rather than over time.

Note: Some authors use the term serial correlation for correlation observed in time series data [i.e., in the sense defined in (*a*)] and autocorrelation for correlation observed in cross-section data [in the sense defined in (*c*)].

14.2. Although in general an AR(m) scheme can be used, the AR(1) scheme has been found to be quite useful in many time series analysis. With the AR(1) scheme, many properties of the OLS estimators can be easily established.

14.3. The consequences are: (1) The OLS estimators are unbiased, but are not efficient. (2) The conventionally estimated standard errors of OLS estimators are biased. (3) As a result, the conventionally computed t and F tests are unreliable, the conventional estimator of σ^2 is biased, and the conventionally computed R^2 may not represent the true R^2.

14.4. The method of generalized difference equation will produce BLUE estimators, provided the first-order autocorrelation parameter, ρ, is known or can be estimated. Also, remember to transform the first observation on the dependent and explanatory variables *a la* Prais-Winsten if the sample size is small.

14.5. These methods are:

(1) The first difference method, where it is assumed that $\rho = 1$

(2) ρ estimated from the Durbin-Watson d as: $\rho \approx 1 - d/2$

(3) ρ estimated from the regression $e_t = \hat{\rho} e_{t-1} + v_t$

(4) The Cochrane-Orcutt iterative procedure

(5) The Cochrane-Orcutt two-step method

(6) Durbin's two-step method

(7) Hildreth-Lu search procedure

(8) Maximum Likelihood method.

14.6. (1) *The graphical method*: There are no particular assumptions made. We simply plot the residuals from an OLS regression chronologically or plot the current residuals on the residuals in the previous time period, if the AR(1) scheme is assumed.

(2) *The Durbin-Watson test*: This test is based on several assumptions, such as (*i*) an intercept term is included in the model; (*ii*) X variables are non-stochastic (fixed in repeated sampling); (*iii*) AR(1) autoregressive scheme; (*iv*) no lagged values of the dependent variable are included as explanatory variables.

(3) *The runs test*: This is a non-parametric test.

14.7. On the Durbin-Watson d test's assumptions, see part (2) of Question 14.6. One drawback of the method is that if the computed d value lies in the uncertain zone, no definite decision can be made about the presence of (first-order) autocorrelation.

14.8. (*a*) *False*. The OLS estimators, although inefficient, are unbiased.

(*b*) *True*. Use the Durbin h test here.

(*c*) *True*. Except for autocorrelation, we are still retaining the other assumptions of the CLRM.

(*d*) *False*. It assumes that $\rho = +1$. If ρ is -1, we regress the two-period moving average of Y on the two-period moving averages of the X variables.

(*e*) *True*. Because the dependent variables in the two models are not the same, the two models cannot be directly compared.

14.9. In small samples, if the first observation is omitted from the transformed regression, the resulting estimators can be inefficient.

PROBLEMS

14.10. The answers are in the last column of the following table:

Sample size	Number of explanatory variables	Durbin-Watson d	Evidence of autocorrelation
25	2	0.83	Yes (positive autocorrelation)
30	5	1.24	Uncertain
50	8	1.98	No autocorrelation
60	6	3.72	Negative autocorrelation
200	20	1.61	Uncertain

14.11. The Swed-Eisenhart results are in the last column of the following table:

Sample size	Number of +	Number of −	Number of runs	Autocorrelation (?)
18	11	7	2	Evidence of autocorrelation
30	15	15	24	Evidence of autocorrelation
38	20	18	6	Evidence of autocorrelation
15	8	7	4	Evidence of autocorrelation
10	5	5	1	Evidence of autocorrelation

14.12. (*a*) The estimated d value is 0.6394. The 5% critical d values are 0.971 and 1.331. Since $0.6394 < 0.971$, there is evidence of positive (first-order) autocorrelation.

(*b*) $\hat{\rho} \approx 1 - \dfrac{d}{2} = 0.6803$

(*c*) <u>Dropping the first observation</u>, we get:

(1) $\hat{Y}_t^* = -1.1230 + 23.3274\,(1/X_t^*)$

$\qquad t = (-0.6210)\quad (3.2700) \qquad\qquad r^2 = 0.5430$

The residuals from this regression, when subjected to the runs test, gave the number of runs as 4, 5 positive and 6 negative residuals.

Retaining the first observation, we obtain:

$$(2) \; \hat{Y}_t^* = -1.8148 + 27.0485 \, (1/X_t^*)$$

$$t = (-0.9793) \quad (3.8169) \qquad\qquad r^2 = 0.5930$$

In the residuals from this regression there were 5 runs, 6 positive and 6 negative residuals.

(d) Based on the runs test, neither regression (1) nor regression (2) seem to have autocorrelation.

Note 1: For X, the transformation is $\dfrac{1}{X_t^*} = \dfrac{1}{X_t} - 0.6803 \left(\dfrac{1}{X}\right)_{t-1}$, given the original format of the independent variable. The intercept in the transformed regressions was entered as $(1-\rho)$.

Note 2: The Prais-Winsten transformation is sensitive to the sample size.

14.13. (a) For $n = 16$ and $k' = 1$, the 5% critical d values are 1.106 and 1.371. Since the computed d of 0.8252 is less than d_L, there is evidence of positive autocorrelation in the data for Model A. For $n = 16$ and $k' = 2$, the 5% critical d values are 0.982 and 1.539. Since the computed d of 1.82 falls between 1.539 (d_U) and 2.461 ($4 - d_U$), we can conclude that there is no evidence of (first-order) positive autocorrelation in Model B.

(b) As this example shows, the Durbin-Watson d can be an indication of a specification error rather than pure auto-correlation.

(c) Although popularly used as a test of first-order autocorrelation, the d statistic can also be used to test for specification errors.

14.14. $\hat{Y}_t = -117.8014 + 0.2608 \, X_t - 0.629 \, X_{t-1} + 0.6562 \, Y_{t-1}$

$t = (-1.8796) \quad (2.6219) \quad (-1.4210) \quad (2.8096) \qquad R^2 = 0.9547$

The estimated ρ is therefore 0.6562.

The results of the second stage regression with transformed X and Y are:

$$\hat{Y}_t^* = -120.3288 + 0.1790 \, X_t^*$$

$$t = (-1.2383) \quad (4.2936) \qquad\qquad r^2 = 0.5060$$

Note: The first observation is included in the analysis *a la* Prais-Winsten. The intercept in the transformed regression has been entered as (1-ρ).

14.15. (a) For $n = 25$ and $k' = 2$, the 5% critical d values are 1.206 and 1.550. Since the computed d value of 0.8755 is below 1.206, there is evidence of positive (first-order) autocorrelation.

(b) Since the Durbin-Watson d test is inappropriate in this case, we cannot trust the computed d value. Perhaps a runs test could be done if the original data were available.

(c) Since in the presence of autocorrelation the conventionally estimated standard errors are biased, it is quite possible that in the original regression these standard errors were underestimated. As a result, the t ratios could be over-estimated. The transformed regression shows this clearly.

(d) See the answer given in (b).

Note: The Durbin-Watson d test assumes an AR(1) scheme. The Durbin two-step procedure implicitly assumes an AR(2) scheme (Why?).

14.16. (a) Using the d value given in the problem, we obtain an estimate of ρ as

$$\left(1 - \frac{1.8624}{2}\right) = 0.0688.$$ Using this value in the h statistic, we obtain:

$$h \approx (0.0688)\sqrt{\frac{17}{1 - 17(0.0403)}} = 0.5055.$$

Obviously, this h value is not statistically significant, suggesting that perhaps there is no autocorrelation in the data. But keep in mind that our sample size is rather small. Therefore, the preceding conclusion must be accepted cautiously.

(b) In autoregressive models like the one in the present example, the d value is generally around 2, which is the d value expected if there is no autocorrelation in the data. Therefore, there is a built-in bias against finding autocorrelation in such models on the basis of the d test.

14.17. (a) $\hat{Y}_t = 10.7849 + 0.0251 X_t$

$t = (1.1666) \quad (7.4671) \qquad\qquad r^2 = 0.7770; \quad d = 0.4618$

(b) For $n = 18$ and $k' = 1$, the 5% critical d values are 1.158 and 1.391. Since the computed d value of 0.4618 is less than 1.158, there is evidence of positive autocorrelation.

(c) $\hat{\rho} = (1 - d/2) = (1 - 0.4618/2) = 0.7691$

(d) *Dropping the first observation*:

$$\hat{Y}_t^* = -26.7007 + 0.0380\, X_t^*$$

$t = (-0.8910) \quad (4.4763) \qquad\qquad r^2 = 0.5719; \quad d = 1.3645$

Retaining the first observation:

$$\hat{Y}_t^* = -21.7121 + 0.0373\, X_t^*$$

$t = (-0.7349) \quad (4.4062) \qquad\qquad r^2 = 0.5842; \quad d = 1.2796$

(e) $\hat{e}_t = 0.8916\, e_{t-1}$

$t = (4.2975) \qquad\qquad\qquad\qquad r^2 = 0.5352$

Note: There is no intercept in this model (Why?). Therefore, $\hat{\rho} = 0.8916$.

Dropping the first observation:

$$\hat{Y}_t^* = -70.3759 + 0.0470\, X_t^*$$

$t = (-1.0784) \; (3.3048) \qquad\qquad r^2 = 0.4213; \quad d = 1.6055$

Keeping the first observation:

$$\hat{Y}_t^* = -66.6092 + 0.0469\, X_t^*$$

$t = (-1.0443) \; (3.3624) \qquad\qquad r^2 = 0.4140; \quad d = 1.5786$

(f) *First difference transformation* (i.e., $\hat{\rho} = 1$):

$$\Delta \hat{Y}_t = 0.0347\, \Delta X_t$$

$t = (2.9824) \qquad\qquad\qquad\qquad r^2 = 0.1048; \quad d = 1.4854$

Note: In the transformed regressions, the intercept was entered as $(1-\rho)$.

(g) The striking result is that in all the transformations given above, whether one includes the first observation or not, there is a difference compared to the original regression. On the basis of the runs test, it can be shown that none of the transformations suffer from the autocorrelation problem.

14.18. (*a*) There is no autocorrelation because the computed d value of 1.67 falls between the 5% critical upper d value of 1.535 ($d_U = 1.535$) and the $4 - d_U$ value of 2.465 ($4 - d_U = 2.465$). The low d value found in Problem 14.17 was probably due to the specification error of omitting the variable, GNP^2.

(*b*) From the regression results, it can be seen that:

$$\frac{dY}{dX} = -0.0454 + 0.0000262X, \text{ and}$$

$$\frac{d^2Y}{dX^2} = 0.0000262$$

If at a given value of X, the first derivative is negative and the second derivative is positive, the slope of Y with respect to X is negative and increasing, that is, the negative slope is becoming less steep as X increases. On the other hand, if at a given X, the first derivative positive and the second derivative is also positive, then Y is increasing at an increasing rate.

(*c*) A priori, one would expect a positive relationship between stock prices and the GNP, although the empirical evidence on this is rather muddy.

14.19. $(Y_t - \rho Y_{t-1}) = B_1(1-\rho) + B_2(X_{2t} - \rho X_{2t-1}) + ... + B_4(X_{4t} - \rho X_{4t-1}) + v_t$

14.20. Expanding (14.5), we obtain:

$$d = \frac{\sum e_t^2 + \sum e_{t-1}^2 - 2\sum e_t e_{t-1}}{\sum e_t^2} = 2(1-\hat{\rho}),$$

using the fact that:

$$\sum e_t^2 \approx \sum e_{t-1}^2 \text{ and } \hat{\rho} = \sum e_t e_{t-1} / \sum e_t^2.$$

14.21. Dividing both numerator and denominator by n^2, we get:

$$\hat{\rho} = \frac{[(1-d/2) + k^2/n^2]}{1 - \frac{k^2}{n^2}}$$

As n tends to infinity, the preceding expression reduces to $(1 - d/2)$.

14.22. At the 5% level, if you routinely apply the Durbin-Watson d test, Model 1 exhibits positive autocorrelation, for the estimated d value lies below the lower critical d value of 1.201 (d_L = 1.201). If you consider model 2, the observed d value of 2.1886 lies between d_U = 1.537 and $4 - d_U$ = 2.463, suggesting that there is positive or negative correlation in the error term. For Model 3, the estimated d of 2.2633 lies between d_U = 1.676 and $4 - d_U$ = 2.324, indicating that this model does not suffer from (first-order) autocorrelation either.

The conclusion that we draw from this exercise is that if you estimate a misspecified model, the observed d value may be more an indication of model specification errors than pure autocorrelation.

14.23. Assign this as a classroom exercise.

14.24. Assign this also as a classroom exercise.

CHAPTER 15

SIMULTANEOUS EQUATION MODELS

QUESTIONS

15.1. The mutual dependence of variables in a regression model leads to the simultaneity problem. Thus in a regression of quantity (Q) on price (P), it is not easy to tell whether we are estimating a demand function or a supply function, since in equilibrium price and quantity are jointly determined.

15.2. An endogenous variable is one whose value is determined within the model, whereas an exogenous variable is one whose value is determined outside the system.

15.3. This is because of the correlation between the error term and one (or more) of the explanatory variables included in an equation in the model.

15.4. Because of the correlation between the error term and the explanatory variable(s) in a given equation within a system of simultaneous equations, the OLS estimators are likely to be biased as well as inconsistent.

15.5. In a reduced form regression, an endogenous variable is expressed solely as a function of predetermined variables (purely exogenous or lagged endogenous) and the error term. A reduced form regression can be consistently estimated by OLS. It is also used to find out whether an equation in a system of simultaneous equations is identified.

15.6. A system of simultaneous equations, has some equations that are identities and some that are structural, or behavioral, in that they depict a particular sector of the economy (e.g., consumption sector, or the production sector).

15.7. For a just or exactly identified structural equation in a system of simultaneous equations, the method of obtaining the estimates of the structural coefficients from the OLS estimates of the reduced form coefficients is known as the method of indirect least squares (ILS).

15.8. By identification of an equation in a system of simultaneous equations we mean whether it is really the thing that we are estimating. Thus, in a regression of quantity on price alone, if we are not sure if it is the demand function or the supply function that we are estimating, then we have an identification problem. It is important, because if we are not sure what we are estimating, what is the point of estimation per se?

15.9. The order condition of identification is a counting method by which we find out what endogenous and predetermined variables are included in a given equation of the system. To be identified, an equation must exclude some variables that are present in the system.

15.10. It means that even if the order condition is satisfied, it may happen that an equation may not be identified. It is like the necessary condition in an optimization problem where by simply setting the first derivative of a function equal to zero we will not be able to tell whether we have obtained a minimum or maximum value of the function at the chosen value of the argument of the function.

15.11. In a system of simultaneous equations, if we cannot estimate the parameters of an equation in the system, that equation is under-identified; if we can obtain unique values of the parameters of that equation, it is exactly identified. However, if we obtain more than one value for one or more parameters of that equation, that equation is over-identified.

15.12. There is no way to estimate such an equation.

15.13. An exactly identified equation can be estimated either by the method of indirect least squares (ILS) or by the method of two-stage least squares (2SLS). Both methods will give the same answer.

15.14. Two-stage least squares is primarily used for estimating the parameters of an over-identified equation.

15.15. Yes, as stated in problem 15.13.

PROBLEMS

15.16. (*a*) The reduced form regressions are:

$$Y_{1t} = \Pi_{10} + \Pi_{11}X_{1t} + \Pi_{12}X_{2t} + w_t$$

$$Y_{2t} = \Pi_{20} + \Pi_{21}X_{1t} + \Pi_{22}X_{2t} + v_t$$

where the Πs are the reduced form coefficients (which are combinations of the structural coefficients, the As and Bs) and where w and v are the reduced form error terms.

(b) Here we have two endogenous variables (the Ys) and two exogenous variables (the Xs). By the order condition, both equations are exactly identified.

(c) Use ILS.

(d) Now the first equation is just identified, but the second is not.

15.17. (a) The first equation in the system is not identified, but the second is. The estimated values of B_1 and B_2 are -5 and 1.5, respectively.

(b) Now both equations are identified by the order condition.

If $A_2 = 0$, we get: $A_1 = 6$; $A_3 = 8$; $B_1 = -5$; $B_2 = 1.5$.

If $A_1 = 0$, we get: $A_2 = 1.5$; $A_3 = -10$; $B_1 = -5$; $B_2 = 1.5$.

15.18. (a) You may want to look up the IS-LM model in any intermediate macroeconomics textbook.

(b) By the order condition of identification, the first equation is not identified but the second is.

(c) First obtain the reduced form regressions, expressing each endogenous variable as a function of the exogenous variable, M in the present case. Estimate these reduced form regressions by the method of ILS.

The results of the reduced form regressions are as follows:

$$\hat{R}_t = 8.0987 - 0.00045 M_t$$

$$t = (6.8868) \quad (-0.8909) \qquad r^2 = 0.0334$$

$$\hat{Y}_t = -215.5029 + 1.7888 M_t$$

$$t = (-2.1294) \quad (41.2459) \qquad r^2 = 0.9867$$

The reader should be able to derive the estimates of the coefficients of the identified equation from the preceding reduced form regressions.

15.19. (a) Now both equations are exactly identified.

(b) The reduced form regressions are as follows:

$$\hat{R}_t = 7.0667 - 0.0058 M_t + 0.0227 I_t$$

$t = (6.5295)\ (-3.0621)\quad (2.9044)\qquad R^2 = 0.3013$

$$\hat{Y}_t = -238.3023 + 1.6696\ M_t + 0.5020\ GDPI_t$$

$t = (-2.1954)\quad (8.7151)\quad (0.6398\qquad R^2 = 0.9869$

From these reduced form regressions, the reader can estimate the parameters of the original structural equations.

(c) The difference between problems 15.18 and 15.19 is that in the latter we could estimate the parameters of each structural equation, whereas in the former we could do it only for the exactly identified equation.

CHAPTER 16

SELECTED TOPICS IN SINGLE EQUATION REGRESSION MODELS

QUESTIONS

16.1. (*a*), (*b*), and (*c*) A dynamic model is a regression model that explicitly allows for intertemporal (i.e., over time) analysis of economic phenomena such as the consumption function, the demand for money function, etc. A dynamic model containing the current values of the explanatory variables as well as their past values is called a *distributed lag model,* whereas a model that includes among the explanatory variables the lagged value(s) of the dependent variable is called an *autoregressive model.*

16.2. Psychological reasons, technological reasons, and institutional reasons can lead to a lagged response of the dependent variable to explanatory variables.

16.3. Such a strategy may be *ad hoc* in that it has no theoretical underpinning. Since the lagged terms are likely to be correlated, every time you add a new term, the model has to be re-estimated. Not only that, but the values of the coefficients already estimated change every time you reestimate the model.

16.4. *True.* Because of collinearity, individual coefficients cannot be estimated precisely, but their sums or differences can be estimated correctly.

16.5. Simplicity at any cost should not be the goal of the model builder. Since the LPM has serious problems, the logit and probit models are the preferred alternatives in regression models that involve dichotomous dependent variables. These models guarantee that the estimated probabilities will be non-negative.

16.6. *True.*

16.7. A spurious regression may result if we regress a nonstationary time series on one or more nonstationary time series. However, such a regression may be meaningful if there is a stable, long-term relationship between these time series, even though individually they are non-stationary. In that case we say that the time series are cointegrated.

PROBLEMS

16.8. (1) $\hat{PCE}_t = -215.1163 + 1.0070 \, PDI_t$

$t = (-6.2591) \quad (63.7248) \qquad\qquad r^2 = 0.9961$

(2) $\hat{PCE}_t = -232.6834 + 0.9827 \, PDI_t + 0.0359 \, PCE_{t-1}$

$t = (-4.7616) \quad (6.3418) \quad (0.2266) \qquad R^2 = 0.9961$

(a) In regression (1), the marginal propensity to consume out of *PDI* is about 1.

(b) From regression (2), the short-run *MPC* is 0.9827 and the long-run *MPC* is $(0.9827 / 0.9641) = 1.0193$. Since the coefficient of the lagged PCE in regression (2) is not statistically significant, for all practical purposes there is no distributed lag effect, that is, the short- and long-run *MPC*s are about the same.

16.9. (1) $\ln\hat{PCE}_t = -0.8839 + 1.1023 \ln PDI_t$

$t = (-6.8130) \quad (65.1424) \qquad\qquad r^2 = 0.9962$

(2) $\ln\hat{PCE}_t = -1.0016 + 1.1409 \ln PDI_t - 0.0238 \ln PCE_{t-1}$

$t = (-4.9827) \quad (6.6975) \quad (-0.1550) \qquad R^2 = 0.9961$

(a) Since we are using a double-log model, all the slope coefficients are elasticities.

(b) From regression (2), the short-run elasticity is 1.1409 and the long-run elasticity is $(1.1409 / 1.0238) = 1.1144$. But statistically there is not much difference between the two (Why?).

16.10. *(a)* Current and lagged capacity utilization rate each has a positive effect on the inflation rate as measured by the GNP deflator. An increasing capacity utilization, *ceteris paribus*, signifies demand pressure, which puts upward pressure on prices. Hence the positive relationship is expected.

(b) The short-run impact is 0.1408 and the long-run impact is found by summing: (0.1408 + 0.2360) = 0.3768.

(c) Yes. For 15 d.f., the 5% (two-tailed) critical t value is 2.131.

(d) Use the R^2 variant of the F test. In the present example, the F value is 19.9725, which is significant beyond the 1% level; the 1% critical F for 2 and 15 d.f. is 6.36 ($F_{2,15} = 6.36$).

(e) Recent data can be found in the latest *Economic Report of the President*.

16.11. We can use the logit model. The results are as follows:

$$\ln\left(\frac{\hat{P}_i}{1-P_i}\right) = -4.8341 + 3.0609 \ln X_i$$

$$t = (-10.8876)\ (11.9046) \qquad r^2 = 0.9793$$

These results show that if the dosage increases by 1%, on the average, the odds in favor of death increase by about 3.06%.

16.12. Here is an illustrative calculation. For $X = 50$, Equation (16.36) gives:

$$\ln\left(\frac{P_i}{1-P_i}\right) = -3.2438 + 0.0792\ (50) = 0.7162$$

Therefore, $\frac{P_i}{1-P_i}$ = antilog(0.7162) = 2.0466.

Solving for P_i, we obtain $P_i = 0.6718$.

16.13. (a) Holding other things constant, if income goes up by a unit, say, a thousand dollars, the log of the odds in favor of restaurant usage goes up by about 0.37 units. Likewise, holding other things constant, the log of the odds in favor of restaurant usage goes down by about -1.1 units if a couple needs a baby sitter. Both these coefficients have the correct signs.

(b) Logit = [-9.456 + 0.3638 (44) – 1.107 (1)] = 5.4442.

(c) Since $\frac{P_i}{1-P_i}$ = antilog(5.4442) = 231.4121, we can solve for P_i in order to get $P_i = 0.9957$.

Therefore, $P_i = 0.9957$ (almost 100%) that a couple with an income of $44,000 and who needs a baby sitter will eat out.

16.14. (*a*) The plots will show that the dividend series is generally upward trending in a rather smooth manner but the profits series, although generally upward trending, shows much more volatility. In both cases, however, the impression one gets is that the two time series are non-stationary.

(*b*) The unit root test was applied to the two series, including the constant and trend terms. The results were as follows:

Dividends

$$\Delta \text{Dividend}_t = 0.5653 + 0.1126\, t - 0.0632\, \text{Dividend}_{t-1}$$

$$t\,(=\tau) = (1.5148) \quad (3.1376) \quad (-2.6395) \qquad R^2 = 0.1480$$

Profits

$$\Delta \text{Profits}_t = 6.5215 + 0.0835\, t - 0.069\, \text{Profits}_{t-1}$$

$$t\,(=\tau) = (2.1541) \quad (1.1420) \quad (-1.7147) \qquad R^2 = 0.0373$$

Note: Δ is the first-difference operator and τ is the Dickey-Fuller tau statistic.

The 1%, 5%, and 10% Augmented Dickey-Fuller critical tau statistic values are -4.0673, -3.4620, and -3.1570, respectively. If the tau values of the lagged terms, Dividend_{t-1} and Profits_{t-1}, are smaller in absolute value than the critical tau values in absolute terms, we conclude that the series under consideration has a unit root, i.e., it is not stationary. Therefore, both our time series are nonstationary.

Note: There is a more advanced version of the unit root Dickey-Fuller (DF) test called the Augmented Dickey-Fuller test (ADF). This is available as an option in *EViews* (it is in the "View" drop-down menu after a variable is opened). The critical values shown above are from there. The ADF critical values can be used because, asymptotically, the DF and ADF tests are the same.

(*c*) If one nonstationary time series (dividends) is regressed on another nonstationary time series (profits), the results are likely to be spurious. However, if the two series are cointegrated, the regression results would not be spurious. Following the discussion in the text, dividends were regressed on profits and the residuals from this regression were subjected to the unit root test, as described in the text, namely, Δe_t was regressed on e_{t-1} (without intercept and trend), where e_{t-1} is the lagged residual term, and the coefficient of the lagged e_{t-1} had a tau (τ) value of 0.9106 in absolute terms, which is below the critical tau values given in (*b*). This suggests that the two time series are not cointegrated. Therefore, the regression of dividends on profits is spurious.

(*d*) Using *EViews*, and applying the Augmented Dickey-Fuller unit root test (with intercept and trend) to the first differences of the two series, it can be observed that the first-differenced time series are stationary. The tau statistic for the appropriate coefficient (lagged value of the first difference of the two time series) is -5.517 (profits) and -6.305 (dividends). In absolute terms, these tau values exceed the critical tau values (in absolute terms) given in (*b*) previously.

16.15. Assign this as a classroom exercise.

16.16. Assign this as a classroom exercise.

16.17. Since the data given in Table 10.10 were artificial, you may have difficulty in estimating the (ungrouped) logit model for these data using the method of maximum-likelihood.

16.18. (*a*) Using *EViews*, we obtained the following LPM regression:

Dependent Variable: Y Sample: 1 32				
Variable	Coefficient	Std. Error	t-Statistic	Prob.
C	-1.498017	0.523889	-2.859419	0.0079
GPA	0.463852	0.161956	2.864054	0.0078
PSI	0.378555	0.139173	2.720035	0.0111
TUCE	0.010495	0.019483	0.538685	0.5944
R-squared	0.415900			
Adjusted R-squared	0.353318			
S.E. of regression	0.388057			

Note: The adjusted R^2 and the standard error of the regression are also shown here.

(b) *EViews* calculates a logit model in a few short steps. In the Table 16-7 workfile, you can proceed as follows:

- Select "Objects" and then "New Object";
- Select "Equation" and click "OK";
- In the Equation Specification Menu, under "Estimation Settings", select "BINARY" from the Method drop-down menu;
- Check the "Logit" box under "Binary estimation method";
- Just type the names of variables in the large Equation Specification box (do not forget the constant C).

The output of the logit function is as follows:

Dependent Variable: Y
Method: ML – Binary Logit
Sample: 1 32

Variable	Coefficient	Std. Error	z-Statistic	Prob.
C	-13.02135	4.931317	-2.640541	0.0083
GPA	2.826113	1.262940	2.237726	0.0252
PSI	2.378688	1.064563	2.234426	0.0255
TUCE	0.095158	0.141554	0.672235	0.5014
S.E. of regression	0.384716	McFadden R-squared		0.374038
Obs with Dep=0	21	Total obs		32
Obs with Dep=1	11			

Note: The conventional R^2 is not very meaningful in models that have a qualitative dependent variable. There are similar measures, collectively known as pseudo R^2. The McFadden R^2 shown above is one such measure. Alternatively, one can use the *Count* R^2 defined in Problem 10.24. When using the *Count* R^2, if the predicted probability is greater than 0.5 we classify it as 1 and if it is less than 0.5 we classify it as 0. Then the number of correct predictions is counted and the *Count* R^2 is computed accordingly. The McFadden R^2 and the *Count* R^2 may sometimes differ substantially. Do keep in mind, however, that goodness-of-fit measures for qualitative dependent variable models are of secondary importance.

(c) The outputs of LPM and Logit models are not directly comparable for reasons discussed in the text, although qualitatively the coefficients have the same signs. In view of the deficiencies of the LPM model, it is better to use the logit or probit model. For instance, in the LPM 5 out of 32 estimated Y values were negative.

16.19. We obtained monthly data on the US / UK exchange rate, number of dollars per pound, for the period January 1980 to July 2004. A graph of the exchange rate series is as follows:

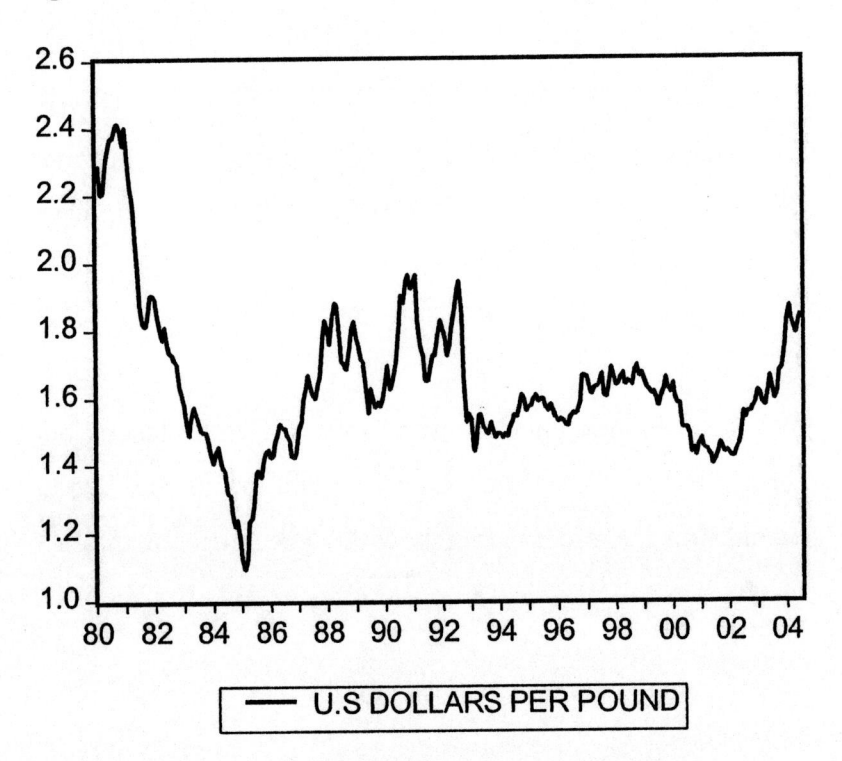

As this graph shows, the exchange rate series seems nonstationary. Using the *EViews* option of the Augmented Dickey-Fuller test (ADF) with trend and intercept term and a lagged difference of 1, we obtain the following results:

ADF Test Statistic	-2.897093	1% Critical Value*	-3.9929
		5% Critical Value	-3.4266
		10% Critical Value	-3.1362
*MacKinnon critical values for rejection of hypothesis of a unit root.			

Since the computed ADF value in absolute terms is less than the 1%, 5% or 10% critical values in absolute terms (i.e., disregarding the sign), we can conclude that the value series is nonstationary. For forecasting purposes, the value series is not useful as it is nonstationary either in its mean value, or variance, or both. If, however, we consider the first difference of the value series, and apply the ADF test with trend and intercept term and a lagged difference of 1, we get the following results:

ADF Test Statistic	−11.13859	1% Critical Value*	−3.9930
		5% Critical Value	−3.4266
		10% Critical Value	−3.1363
*MacKinnon critical values for rejection of hypothesis of a unit root.			

Since the absolute value of the ADF test statistic is greater (in absolute terms) than the 1%, 5% or 10% critical ADF values (in absolute terms), we can conclude that it is the first differences of the value series that are stationary, Therefore, the first-differenced time series can be used for forecasting.

Note: The *EViews* unit root test option allows for testing on the level of the series, its first difference, and its second difference. See the unit root test menu. You can also experiment with lagged differences other than 1.